More Than
Silver or Gold

Homilies of a Stewardship Priest

D1566603

More Than
Silver or Gold
Homilies of a Stewardship Priest

Daniel J. Mahan

Saint Catherine of Siena Press
Excellence in Catechesis
In Faithfulness to Rome

Saint Catherine of Siena Press
4812 North Park Avenue
Indianapolis, IN 46205
888-232-1492
www.saintcatherineofsienapress.com
www.morethansilverorgold.com

Nihil obstat: Rev. Dennis M. Duvelius, F.S.S.P.
                  Censor Librorum

Imprimatur: Rev. Msgr. Joseph F. Schaedel
                  Vicar General and Moderator of the Curia

Given at Indianapolis, Indiana, on June 20, 2005.

The *Nihil Obstat* and *Imprimatur* are official declarations that a book or pamphlet is free of doctrinal or moral error. No implication is contained therein that those who have granted the *Nihil obstat* and *Imprimatur* agree with the content, opinions, or statements expressed.

All Scripture quotations, unless otherwise indicated, are taken from the Catholic Edition of the Revised Standard Version of the Bible, © 1965, 1966 by the Division of Christian Education of the National Council of the Churches of Christ in the United States of America. Used by permission. All rights reserved.

Excerpts from the English translation of the *Catechism of the Catholic Church* for use in the United States of America ©1994, United States Catholic Conference, Inc. – Libreria Editrice Vaticana. Used with permission.

Additional acknowledgments may be found on page 182.

Printed in the United States of America.

ISBN-13:   978-0-9762284-9-3
ISBN-10:   0-9762284-9-1

Library of Congress Control Number: 2005928105

Cover photos: Interior of St. Louis Catholic Church, Batesville, Indiana (1870). Photography courtesy of Linda Fullenkamp, Hillenbrand Graphic Communications, Batesville; Engleking's Creative Photography, Batesville.

Contents

Foreword

When my good friend Father Dan Mahan asked me to write the foreword for his book, *More than Silver or Gold: Homilies of a Stewardship Priest,* I said "Yes" as a favor to him. Then I set out to read the book. As I did so, that favor ceased to be a job and became a joy! I found *More than Silver or Gold* to be a fascinating book with great examples and a dynamic text that kept me going page after page. It's a really valuable find, a guide to stewardship that is both practical and inspirational.

Stewardship is plagued by a number of misconceptions, one of the most widespread being that stewardship is merely a guise for the Church to get additional, much-needed money. Financial support for the Church is critical, but that's neither the first nor the most important component of stewardship.

In Chapter One, Father Mahan confronts that misconception and examines stewardship as *a way of life, a spirituality.* The result: one of the best articulations of what Catholic stewardship is all about.

Paramount in our spirituality of stewardship is the time that we give to God in prayer. Precious too is our time spent with our family and with the Church. We are challenged to share our talents, bringing about the good things of the Kingdom in our homes, parishes, and community. We are to support not just our Church, but our community, and the many agencies that carry out the work of the Gospel.

In Chapter Two, Father Mahan hits a key ingredient to becoming a successful steward – *conversion* – and in doing so he refutes yet another misconception.

Some interpret conversion as a once-in-a-lifetime movement towards Christ and His way of life. They liken it to the experience of Paul, knocked to the ground, blinded by the light, mesmerized by the voice of Jesus. Instantaneously Paul

7

was changed, welcomed baptism, and became the holy apostle we all remember.

Conversion is indeed a grace-filled process, but unlike Paul's experience, it's usually more ordinary. It takes time to become a saintly steward, to live with increasing generosity, overcoming our inborn tendency to consume rather than to contribute. The universal call to holiness summons every one of us to come closer to Jesus through a saintly life. By His grace, Jesus sets the steward on a gradual and grace-ful path to communion with Him, in holiness of life.

Communion, presented in Chapter Three, is another key to the heart of stewardship, for Catholic stewards are encouraged to become active in their parishes and the wider Church community. Participation makes the difference, strengthening the bonds of one to another, bringing forth a thriving parish. With communion also comes a deep appreciation for the gift of the Church: folks come to know the Eucharist as ***the treasure worth more than silver or gold***, the gift that creates the unity of the Body of Christ.

The final chapter is dedicated to the concept of ***mission***. "Go, the Mass is ended" is the dismissal that the faithful hear as the celebration of the Mass is concluded. Stewards are reminded that they are now to share the Good News with others and to work at making ours a culture of life. Father Mahan is correct in suggesting that stewardship is a marvelous energizer to move mission ahead in the Church.

And so, I invite you to set out as I did – to read, to savor, to ***act upon*** these homilies presented in *More than Silver or Gold.* May Father Mahan's words draw you more deeply into a generous life of Catholic stewardship, united with the One who cannot be outdone in generosity.

Most Reverend James P. Keleher, S.T.D.
Archbishop Emeritus, Archdiocese of Kansas City in Kansas
The Solemnity of the Most Sacred Heart of Jesus
June 3, 2005

Preface

Stewardship is a misunderstood word in the Church today. According to the Bishops of the United States and the International Catholic Stewardship Council (ICSC), stewardship is **a way of life** that holds the **promise for far-reaching renewal** within the Church. In contrast, others claim that stewardship is merely a mercenary euphemism: secular fundraising in sheep's clothing.

I subscribe to the former point of view. Stewardship has been eminently helpful to me as a priest, as a pastor, and as one committed to stewardship education. Having been privileged to serve as pastor of three different parishes since 1992, I have witnessed **the benefits of stewardship to parishioners and parish alike.** In fact, the practice of good stewardship led the parish of Saint Rose of Lima in Franklin, Indiana, to found a new Catholic elementary school. Parishioners at St. Luke in Indianapolis practiced stewardship so faithfully that they established both a Perpetual Adoration Chapel and engaged in an expansion and upgrade of the parish facilities. Good stewards at my present parish, Saint Louis in Batesville, Indiana, work and pray together to form a tightly knit parish community that supports a host of ministries and services, including an expanding parish school.

Nor is this a local phenomenon. While he was still a cardinal, **our Holy Father Pope Benedict XVI** said, "The promotion of the practice of stewardship is important for the mission of the Church and for the spiritual well-being of each Christian. Everyone benefits from the sacrificial gift one makes of his time, talent, and treasure."[1] My participation in ICSC over this past decade and the opportunity to teach

---

[1] From the letter of His Eminence Joseph Cardinal Ratzinger of June 20, 1997, to His Excellency The Most Reverend James Patrick Keleher, S.T.D., Archbishop of Kansas City in Kansas and Episcopal Moderator of the National Catholic Stewardship Council.

stewardship in over forty dioceses bears this out. Without exception, I have found that the stewardship movement is taking hold to the Church's great benefit.

✠

If we define a steward as one who is a caretaker of another's property, then a Catholic steward embraces and embodies the truth that our talents and opportunities are blessings entrusted to us by our God who is gracious, munificent, and incomparably generous. So generous, in fact, is the Father that He spares not His only-begotten Son that we might have life and have it to the full.

Our Lord Jesus is the priceless gift of the Father, the gift worth infinitely more than silver or gold (1 Peter 1:18). The Catholic steward lives with the Lord Jesus as the pivot point of all he or she does and is, most especially by encountering Him frequently in the Holy Eucharist. It is there that the self-giving of Jesus is perpetuated, His perfect sacrifice upon the Cross made present under the form of bread and wine.

In Holy Communion the faithful receive the great gift that rust cannot tarnish nor moth destroy nor thief steal away, the gift worth so much ***more than silver or gold,*** the Body and Blood, Soul and Divinity of the Lord. He gives Himself to us so intimately in order that we might be changed, fashioned more closely into His image and likeness. We are converted. We become Who we receive.

The connection, then, between a life of Catholic stewardship and vibrancy in the Church arises from profound commitment to our Eucharistic Lord Jesus. Catholic stewardship is lived most fully when intimacy with the Eucharistic Lord effects visible change in one's daily life. Thus, the good steward lives ever conscious of the goodness of God, and is defined by the virtues of responsibility and generosity: "Without cost you have received, without cost you are to give." (Mt 10:8)

In *More than Silver or Gold,* I put forth my understanding of stewardship and my vision for the future of the Church.

Chapter One introduces the fundamental elements of stewardship as a way of life, expressed concretely in the sharing of the gifts of time, talent, and treasure. I begin with "Stewardship: A Practical Spirituality," an essay distilled from a popular talk that I have delivered many times in recent years. Following the essay is a triptych of homilies preached at St. Louis Parish in 2002 during our annual stewardship commitment weekend.

Chapters Two, Three, and Four present the theology and spirituality of stewardship applied to the everyday life of the Church; specific themes include respect for the dignity of the human person, marriage and family life, and growth in virtue and holiness. Each of the three fruits evident in a stewardship parish are depicted in separate chapters: greater *conversion* of heart (Chapter Two), an increased sense of *communion* in the Church (Chapter Three), and a more vibrant witness of one's Christian *mission* in the world (Chapter Four).

Each autumn, I devote three consecutive weekends to speaking to my parishioners about stewardship of time, talent, and treasure, with the Gospel of the day serving as a springboard. The selections in *Chapter Five* are drawn from those annual homilies.

Feel free to read this book as you would an anthology, beginning at any point and skipping around as you wish. My hope is that you will find this collection to be a source of inspiration, education, and motivation in living the life of a good steward of God's many gifts.

While I have made every effort to convert preached homilies into the written word, nevertheless you will discover several instances of expressions that are more suited for the pulpit than for a manuscript. For this I beg your indulgence.

This book would not have been written except for the encouragement, assistance, and prayers of:

Those who have heard me preach over the years and encouraged me to make my homilies available in writing;

The International Catholic Stewardship Council, whose leaders and members have so graciously invited me to events throughout North America and the Caribbean to teach stewardship as a way of life;

My dear friends who have helped with the production of this book, especially my mentor in stewardship, Mr. Daniel Conway of RSI Catholic Services Group; my theological advisers in St. Louis, Dr. Lawrence J. Welch of Kenrick Seminary and Dr. Shawn McCauley Welch of the Pope Paul VI Institute; my proofreaders, Brenda Henry and Teresa Hartley; those who shared their professional talents to produce the accompanying CD, Guy Sallade, Marty Doucette, Ariel Doucette, and Mike Weiler; and my closest collaborator Jean Zander of Saint Catherine of Siena Press, who with her husband Tony and children Eileen, Will, and Kevin, gave me invaluable help along the way; and most of all,

Our Lord Jesus Christ, to whom I never cease addressing prayers of thanks for calling me to the priesthood, the greatest adventure and most profound joy of my life.

Reverend Daniel J. Mahan, S.T.L.
June 29, 2005
The Solemnity of Saints Peter and Paul

CHAPTER ONE
STEWARDSHIP: A WAY OF LIFE

✠

Stewardship: A Practical Spirituality

Each year, I have many opportunities to travel the country and speak about **stewardship**. *Often I'm invited by a parish priest to preach the Masses on a given weekend, and when I announce to the congregation the topic for my homily, usually I can see a few eyes roll! People are convinced that I'm going to talk about stewardship as a word beginning with the capital letter "S" with a line running down the middle: $ What follows is my best attempt to set the record straight about stewardship.*

Let us be clear: Stewardship is neither a gimmick nor a ruse. Stewardship is *a way of life* that is *deeply rooted in the person of Jesus Christ,* who came to teach us how to live. He came not to do His own will, but the will of the One who sent Him. He came not to be served, but to serve. He came to give His life as a ransom for the many.[2]

Jesus came to teach us everything that we need to know about life. Through the way of life that is stewardship, He draws us closer to Himself, day by day; we build a sense of communion in our Church; and we come to understand more clearly that *God has given each of us something to do that no one else on earth can do.* No one can be the parent or the grandparent or the member of your parish the way that you are called to be. Through stewardship Jesus

---

[2] Cf. Matthew 20:28.

makes clear to each of us our individual mission in the Church, giving us the grace to live *stewardship as a way of life, a way of holiness, a spirituality.*

What is a good steward?

When the American bishops wrote their 1992 pastoral letter, *Stewardship: A Disciple's Response*,[3] they defined a good steward as one who embodied four specific qualities:

1) *A good steward is one who is grateful,* thanking God daily for the blessings he or she has received. A good steward never stops saying "thank you."

2) *A good steward is one who is responsible* and accountable with the blessings that God has bestowed, not only using them prudently, but also making sure that they do not atrophy. It's that way with some gifts, isn't it? Think about the gift of music. A musician needs to take lessons, working with the gift of music lest it atrophy and fade away.

It's that way with every gift, especially the gift of faith. Parents are good stewards when they care for, protect, and nurture their children's natural aptitude for faith, beginning in the tender years of early childhood.

3) *A good steward is one who shares God's gifts out of a sense of love and justice.* A good steward knows that it is better to give than to receive,[4] for in giving we receive far more than we could ever have imagined.

4) *Finally, a good steward is one who makes a return to the Lord with increase.* Remember the parable of the stewards to whom the master had entrusted the silver pieces? They had to render an account of their stewardship. One day you and I will have to stand in accountability before the

---

[3] *Stewardship: A Disciple's Response: A Pastoral Letter on Stewardship,* United States Conference of Catholic Bishops, 1992.
[4] Cf. Acts 20:35.

judgment seat of God. And God will ask: "What did you do with all the time that you had? What did you do with all the gifts that I gave you? *What did you do with your life?"*

Hopefully, we will be able to say, "Lord, I tried to *thank you* every day. I tried to be *responsible* with those gifts. And I tried to *share* those gifts with others. Please God, may He respond, "Well done, good and faithful steward. Come and share your Master's joy."[5]

Stewardship: Involvement and Commitment

When we promote stewardship as a way of life, when we encourage within other people those virtues of gratitude, responsibility, and generosity, some wonderful things happen in our parishes. We find that parishioners:

- *are more grateful and more constructive,* even in their criticism;
- *get involved and become committed* to the life of the Church; and
- *live a more vibrant Christian witness* to the world-at-large.

That having been said, *I want to be clear:* stewardship is *not* confined to the portion of a person's time or income that is given back to the parish. Those *are* good things. The Church needs people who are actively involved and committed in the parish. But the true aim of stewardship is toward *a more vibrant witness "out in the world."*

The primary place where the lay apostolate is to be engaged is out in the world. It's in the family, in the marketplace, at work, at school. It's in the culture, striving to make a difference in the law of the land and in the institutions that form the culture. It is, as our late Holy Father Pope John

---

[5] Cf. Matthew 25:21.

Paul II was so fond of saying – **helping to transform the culture of death into a culture of life.**

That's the goal of stewardship. Stewardship is **not** promoted just to make sure that the parish needs are met, but to engage and energize every Catholic for service, **starting in the family** and **then extending** into the wider world.

Stewardship: A Way of Life

My introduction to stewardship came when I was assigned to my first pastorate, a parish of 500 families just outside the city of Indianapolis. I was committed to strengthening the fiscal position of the parish and searched for **a program** to help us do just that. A friend suggested that I look at stewardship. And I did. I researched it, found a nice manual on stewardship, and did everything as I was instructed. I spent a month communicating about stewardship, preaching homilies, sending letters, distributing brochures. **Finally there was a commitment card,** asking people to respond with an intention to give of their time, their talent, and their treasure.

You know what happened? It worked! The collections rose dramatically. The volunteer lists swelled. People started showing up for things like our clean-up, paint-up, fix-up days. In fact one Saturday they descended upon the parish like an army. They just took over the parish grounds that afternoon, cleaning, painting and fixing. It was delightful!

Well, when things in the parish turn around quickly, the chancery takes notice. A representative from the chancery met with our parish council to learn more about our program – what we were doing, why it was working. At that meeting, the representative asked two questions that I'll never forget.

The first question was "Do you like stewardship?" Naturally, everyone responded, "Oh, yes! Of course!"

Then the second question: "Would you still like stewardship even if the collections hadn't gone up so much?" And to a person, each one in that room responded, "Yes!"

It was at that point that I realized that stewardship is not a program, but that it is a dynamic, a way of life.

The council members started to tell their stories. Stories like the one of a man who began the practice of writing his check for the offertory as soon as he deposited his paycheck from the factory. And the two teenage boys who prevailed upon their parents to disconnect the cable TV so the family could give more to the Church.

And the story of the doctor who heard a homily about stewardship and told the priest, "Father, before this Mass today I have never thought about the ability to practice medicine as being a gift from God."

The message of stewardship resonates in the hearts of parishioners, for it is a practical spirituality, a way of holiness.

Stewardship: A Practical Spirituality

Spirituality is a bit hard to define, so I'd prefer to illustrate the meaning through a little story.

There once were two fish who lived in a small pond. The older fish spent his days swimming serenely, while the younger fish darted around, peeking under fallen branches and behind rocks. Finally, the older fish asked, "What are you doing? I'm getting tired just looking at you." The younger one explained, "I'm looking for water! I've heard that it's really good for us fish. We can't live without it." The older fish retorted, "You dummy! You're swimming in it! Above you, below you, around you – it's all over." And the younger fish said, "You mean this water that's supposed to be

so good for us is *just right here?* It can't be that simple."
And he swam away, continuing his search for water.

The question for us is: *where do we look for God?* Do
we search hither and yon? Do we think that we have to scale
a high peak and seek out a guru? Or do *we recognize the
presence of God in His creation:* in the majesty of sunlight
reflecting off mountain snow, the sparkle of a mountain
stream, the beauty of the flora and fauna? Do we recognize
the presence of God in His most prized creation, man and
woman, created in His image and likeness?

Do we recognize God in history? Our God is not one
who keeps His distance, but rather enters into the human
experience: sending a way of freedom to His enslaved Chosen
People; sending prophets to foretell the promise of a new
covenant; and most especially sending His own Son, the
Word made flesh, to dwell among us. Our Lord Jesus
stretched out His arms on the cross, suffered and died for our
sinfulness, and opened the gates of heaven to us.

Do we recognize God in this age of the Holy Spirit,
where we experience the presence of God through His bride,[6]
the Church, and through her sacraments, especially the great
sacrament of the Holy Eucharist? In this gift of His Body
and Blood, Soul and Divinity, Jesus keeps His solemn
promise, "I am with you always, even until the end of the
age."[7]

Do we recognize God where He can be found? Too
often we say, "God can't be found amidst the regular course
of our lives. It can't be that simple."

*Stewardship is an invitation for people to recognize
the presence of God in their lives:* in their families, in their
work, in their associations with the Church, in their reception

---

[6] Cf. Revelation 19:7; 21:2; 21:9; 22:17.
[7] Cf. Matthew 28:20.

of the sacraments, in the work that they do for the building up of the Kingdom.

Time, Talent, and Treasure

As we recognize the presence of God in our lives, we set out to live the spirituality of stewardship in terms of *time, talent, and treasure.* I want to say a word about each of the three.

Stewardship of Time

Some people say "time is money", right? Well, it's not. It's much more valuable than money! We've all had the experience of wasting money on poor purchases or bad decisions. We recover from that, but not so with time. Time once spent can never be recovered. Every day, every hour is precious. And we know neither the day nor the hour that God will call us home to Him.[8] God gives us today, but He does not promise us tomorrow.

Those principles are the message of stewardship that I need to hear over and over again: Make sure that what's important gets done first. Make sure that prayer is at the top of the list, not "when there is time for it," or else there will never be time for it. Make sure that family responsibilities are fulfilled. *Make sure that we take care of the things that matter.*

That's what stewardship of time is all about. It's more than inviting people to spend a few hours volunteering in the parish. It's helping people to look at their lives, 24 hours each day, as an opportunity to serve the Lord and to build up the Kingdom.

---

[8] Cf. Matthew 24:36.

Stewardship of Talent

We can't think of stewardship of talent only in terms of what we can do to help out around the parish. **Talent is the passion that people have for doing what is good.** I think of the people in my parish who are passionate about the cause of the poor, who are passionate about pro-life issues. In bringing their passion to all that they do, they make a difference. That's great stewardship of talent.

Stewardship of Treasure

This is the one we want to avoid at all costs! It's been said that if a priest is pastor of a parish for 30 years and he mentions money **once,** when he dies his parishioners will walk past his tombstone, shaking their heads, muttering, "There rests the priest who **always** talked about money!"

Money is so personal. We don't speak in public about how much money we have in the bank or what our house is worth. We don't do that! It's too personal.

Jesus knows this. Take careful note: it's not the priest who keeps bringing up the subject of money in church, it's the Lord! Listen to the parables of Jesus as they are told through the Church year. About half of the parables of Jesus have to do with money or with material possessions: for example, the lost coin, the widow's mite, the buried treasure in the field, the Good Samaritan who gives the two silver pieces to the innkeeper, and so on.

Jesus keeps talking about money because he knows how personal it is. He knows that sometimes money is **too** important and can actually keep us from the fullness of life with Him. Remember the rich young man who went to see Jesus? [9] That young man knew that in order to have eternal

---

[9] Cf. Matthew 19:16-22.

life he had to keep the commandments, but then he asked Jesus, "What more must I do?" Jesus looked at the man *with love* and He said, "Sell what you possess and give it to the poor ... and come, follow me."[10] We are told that the rich young man went away sad, because he had so many possessions.[11]

Up to that point, those possessions had brought great joy and comfort to his life. Now they were a source of sadness. In going away from Jesus that day, the young man missed out on the opportunity of a lifetime – *the invitation to follow the Master* – all because he had so much "stuff."

We speak about stewardship of treasure *not* because of the need of the parish, but because of *our own need to give.* No matter what windfall a parish might experience – striking oil in the parking lot, coming upon a winning lottery ticket, inheriting a sizeable bequest – the parish must *still* emphasize stewardship of treasure. Why? Because *stewardship of treasure is not about giving to a need, but rather it is about the need to give,* a need to make sure that material possessions do not dominate our lives.

Stewardship and the Church

We speak of stewardship not as a program, but as a way of life, a way of holiness. Still it's a relatively new word in our Catholic lexicon. A new word, yes, but *not a new spirituality,* for it is as old as the Church herself.

We recall the Acts of the Apostles, where we learn that the apostles kept a common purse to take care of the needs

---

[10] Matthew 19:21.

[11] Our brothers and sisters in the Eastern Church honor the rich young man as a saint, knowing that Jesus does give second chances and trusting that the young man changed his mind.

of the poor.[12] Those early Christians were recognized by this distinguishing mark of charity.[13] That's good stewardship.

We recall the thin red line of the blood of the martyrs, blood shed by men and women of faith. They loved the Lord Jesus and remained faithful, not counting the cost. They gave their lives for the sake of the Gospel. That's good stewardship.

We recall the missionary men and women who left behind family and homeland, never to see them again, all to ensure that the Gospel was preached in new lands. That's good stewardship.

We recall the immigrants who came to this side of the ocean, many of them carrying little more than the clothing on their backs, but they made their home and made sure that the Catholic Church was established for the benefit of generations to come. That's good stewardship.

We recall the American Catholics of the World War II generation who sacrificed for new schools, new parishes, and new Catholic hospitals – to make sure that a strong Catholic presence would endure. That's good stewardship.

I've been fortunate as a pastor to see the message of stewardship resonate in the hearts of people in three very different parishes. People respond to that message positively because they know that *this is the way* that the Church has been built up throughout the years. It's how the Catholic faith has been lived out vibrantly in every age, in every place, in every generation.

When the history of our generation of Catholics is written, I pray that we will be known for our good stewardship. May it be said of us, "What good stewards they were! They faced economic uncertainty and shifting

---

[12] Cf. Acts 2:44,45; Acts 4:32,34,35.
[13] Cf. John 13:35.

demographics. They faced threats to the Church from without and scandal from within. And yet they kept investing themselves in the life of the Church. They kept praying. They kept coming to Mass. They kept participating. They kept giving their life's blood for the sake of the Church, and through their efforts and the grace of God, *the world around them started to change.* Ever gradually, the culture of death became a culture of life."

Please God may that be said of us. That's the vision of stewardship. That's what we mean when we say stewardship is a way of life, a practical spirituality.

A Stewardship Triptych:

Three Homilies about
Time, Talent and Treasure

I preached these homilies over three consecutive Sundays as part of the annual renewal of stewardship in the parish. I do this every year because the message is so critical to the vitality of the Church and the holiness of Her members.

The Invitation

The homily that follows gives an overview to stewardship as a way of life. Its starting point is the Gospel of the day, the parable of the king who found only apathy when he invited his subjects to a wedding.[14]

Over the course of the next three weeks I will be speaking about stewardship of time, talent, and treasure. This is the time of year for the harvest: *a time for us to be grateful* for our many blessings and to be conscious of our responsibility to share those blessings with our Church, both in the parish and through the United Catholic Appeal.[15]

Stewardship is a misunderstood word. But stewardship is neither a gimmick nor a fundraising scheme. Rather, *stewardship is a way of life rooted in the teachings and the person of Jesus Christ.* All of us are called not only to be stewards, but also to be *good* and *faithful* stewards, in imitation of the Lord Himself.

---

[14] Cf. Matthew 22:1-14.
[15] The United Catholic Appeal is the annual fund of the Archdiocese of Indianapolis.

We begin our discussion of stewardship with today's Gospel, the parable of the wedding invitations.

I'm not sure about you, but I don't fully understand the etiquette of wedding invitations. I can tell when I have received one in the mail by the sheer weight of the envelope. Then when I open it I discover one envelope inside another envelope, with a third envelope inside all of that! And if anyone knows the reason for the tissue paper inside, please tell me!

Even if I don't understand why wedding invitations are printed the way they are, I do understand the significance of the occasion. A wedding is so important that one could hardly get by with extending a casual invitation. The occasion demands formality. A wedding invitation deserves to be answered, the RSVP card returned. When one accepts an invitation to attend a wedding, that guest has an obligation to dress and behave appropriately for the occasion. The bride and groom and their parents deserve no less.

So we are astonished at what happens in today's parable. The wedding invitations are sent by a king, no less! Imagine what that wedding reception will be like. Not something to be missed! And yet the king's invitations are ignored, his messengers assaulted. When the guests finally arrive some are improperly dressed. Imagine the gall! Imagine the indignity that the king suffered.

What does this parable have to do with stewardship? The king in the story is, of course, **God the Father, who invites each of us** to share in the "wedding feast," the love of His only begotten Son, our Lord Jesus.[16] The invitation is extended freely, graciously, and generously. No one here deserves to be invited to a wedding by an earthly king, let alone the King of heaven and earth. And yet so great is the

---

[16] Cf. Revelation 19:9.

Father that He never stops calling us to share in the joy, happiness, and love – *the wedding feast* – of Jesus.

The invitation to the wedding feast is the magnanimous gift of the Father. The question is, *"How do I respond?"*

- *Am I grateful* for the gift of faith, or do I take my faith for granted?
- *Am I faithful* in my responsibilities as a follower of Jesus, or am I negligent in my duties?
- *Am I generous* in sharing with the Church my blessings that come from the hands of our merciful and munificent God?

These are the questions that a good steward must ask on a regular basis.

Stewardship is about our response to God's invitation. Stewardship is *an attitude*, a stance in life of expressing through our daily living our gratitude to the Lord for all of His blessings. Stewardship is *a way of life* that calls us to ongoing conversion of heart and practical, concrete changes in our lives. Stewardship is what *we do* after we say "We Believe."

Let's be clear: stewardship is *not* about what we do with a portion of our time, talent, or treasure. It is *not* just about the portion we give to the Church. Rather, *stewardship is about how we live our lives in total.*

The key question is *not,* "how much time do I give to God?" *but instead,* "from how much of my time do I exclude God?"[17]

The key question is *not,* "how much am I putting into the collection basket?" *but instead,* "how am I using all of the gifts of treasure at our disposal?" It is a matter of

---

[17] That's a pretty good definition of sin, isn't it? Excluding God from some aspect of our lives.

knowing the critical difference between what I own and what owns me.

Stewardship is about how we use *all of our gifts* for the building up of the Kingdom of God. Still, we are mindful of our particular responsibilities to our parish and our archdiocesan church.

Our parish has been built up by faithful stewards every day since 1868. Seven generations of men and women of faith built this church and school, and have maintained and expanded it to keep up with the needs of the day. These *generations of stewards* have given of their time and talent to build up a community in which the seeds of faith could grow and develop. The sacrifices of those parishioners and their generous stewardship of their gifts has made St. Louis a parish in which we can take great pride, a parish that draws people closer to Jesus and the bonds of the Catholic Church.

We owe a debt of gratitude to those good and faithful stewards, a debt we repay, in part, by our involvement and commitment in the life of our Church. We can *only* be the parish the Lord is calling us to be if *every* parishioner responds generously to the Lord's invitation. We can do the Lord's work *only* if we are committed to good stewardship of our time, talent, and treasure.

I will speak more directly about stewardship over the next two weeks. Parishioners will receive several mailings as well. I emphasize stewardship for three reasons:

First, our parish needs it. We depend upon good stewardship to do what the Lord is calling us to do.

Second, each of us needs it. We need to give of ourselves for the good of the Church, for it is in giving that we receive. So often those who give generously find that they receive far more in return.

Third, the Father is expecting a reply to His invitation. The Father invites each of us personally, with a hand-written invitation, as it were. He wants us to be fully present to share in the love of His Son, a love that is made present in manifold ways in the life of the Church, right here at St. Louis Parish.

By our sharing in the Lord's Body and Blood may the grace of this Sacrament inspire us to be more committed to serving Him through good stewardship of our time, talent, and treasure.

✠ **The Twenty-eighth Sunday in Ordinary Time (A)**
October 13, 2002

The Golf Balls

Preaching about stewardship of time and talent is good for the Church primarily because those who listen have an opportunity to think about what is truly important in their lives, and to make adjustments accordingly.

Last week I spoke about stewardship as a way of life: *a way of life deeply rooted in the person and teachings of Jesus*, a concrete response to God's invitation to be generous in sharing our blessings of time, talent, and treasure, all for the up-building of the Church.

I speak today specifically about the *stewardship of time and talent,* and I do so from two angles.

The first angle is obvious: our parish depends upon the time and talent of many generous people. Those who give so graciously of their time and talent are the pillars of our community. Just think about all that goes on in our parish and those who work so diligently in religious education, in RCIA,[18] in taking Holy Communion to the sick and shut-ins, in working with the youth, in serving the poor

---

[18] The Rite of Christian Initiation of Adults.

and less fortunate in the name of the parish, in assisting with the liturgy as lectors, ushers, choir members. The list goes on and on! These generous stewards of time and talent are literally the life blood of our parish. And so to those who serve so often and so well, *please accept my thanks.* Our parish would not be as vibrant without you.

To those who are not yet involved in parish activities, please consider getting involved. Many opportunities can be found in reading the bulletin and in listening to the parish announcements. These announcements are made not for the person sitting behind you, but for *you* to consider prayerfully. In addition, a time and talent sheet that will be sent to you by mail will give you an opportunity to sign up. Please know that we will do our best to respond quickly to those who want to get involved.

Giving your time and talent to the Church is a great way to stay connected to the faith and to help build up the Kingdom of God. *Look for opportunities to get involved and you will find them.*

This is one way to speak about stewardship of time and talent – *from the perspective of the parish's need* for those gifts. Let's remember that stewardship is *not* just about the portion that we give to the Church. Stewardship is about how we use *all our time, talent and treasure* for the glory and honor of God.

You see *the second angle* from which I speak deals with the *art of stewardship of time*, or "time management", as it is called in the secular world. Corporations spend a great amount of money sending their employees to time management seminars or bringing in the experts to give advice. Why do they do this? Because time is money! It behooves a corporation to have employees who are skilled at using their time wisely and efficiently.

A professor once wanted to make that point with his class about the importance of time. He produced from beneath the podium a very large pickle jar filled to the brim with golf balls. He asked the class, "Is the jar full?" They responded, "Yes." And he said, "Well, watch this."

Pulling from his briefcase a bag of pebbles, he poured the pebbles into the jar so that they filled in the empty spaces around the golf balls. Again he asked, "Is the jar full?" Again they responded, "Yes."

He pulled out from underneath the podium a bag of sand and two cans of beer. He first poured the sand into the jar and then followed with the beer, until the jar overflowed.

Then he announced, "Now I tell you the jar is full. And heed the moral. I want you to recognize that the jar represents your life. The golf balls are important things: your family, your spouse, your health, your children, your friends, your passions. If everything was lost and only they remained, your life would still be full. The pebbles are the other things that matter a lot, like your job, your house, your car. And the sand is everything else, the small stuff.

"If you put the sand in the jar first, there's no room for the pebbles or the golf balls. The same goes for your life. If you spend all your time and energy on the small stuff you will never have room for the things that are important to you. So pay attention to the things that are critical for your happiness, play with your children, take time to get medical check-ups, take your spouse out dancing, play another 18. There will always be time to go to work, clean the house, and give a dinner party.

"Take care of the golf balls first, the things that really matter. Set your priorities. The rest is just sand."

"One perceptive student raised her hand and she said, "Professor, what about the two cans of beer?" And he said, "I'm glad you asked. It just goes to show you that no matter how busy your life might be, you'll always have time for a couple of beers!"

Putting the golf balls in first. This is an important lesson about stewardship of time that everyone needs to hear on a regular basis. **What are the golf balls, the important things in our lives?** Do we always remember to make it a priority to spend time with God through prayer and the sacraments? To spend time with our families? To spend time engaged in the life of the Church so that our lives might be rooted more firmly in faith?

These are the things that must go in first in our lives — because we know all too well that our lives can fill up too easily with "pebbles and sand", such as watching mindless television shows, playing endless hours of video games or surfing the internet, engaging in idle gossip, and frequenting places that do marriage and family no good at all.

Stewardship of time is about paying attention to three important things in life.

First, it's about making sure that we are connecting with the Lord through faithful prayer and regular participation in the sacraments of the Church. **Second,** it's about making sure that we are spending time with our families – and not just the so-called "quality time" but the "quantity time" that really makes a difference. **Third,** it's about making sure that our lives are anchored firmly in our community of faith by allowing our lives to revolve around the worship of the Lord and the activities of our parish.

These three go together and I pray that these three come together for every family here: that healthy marriages and strong families might be built up. May this growth take place through the power of prayer and the sacraments, through the commitment to spending time together, by being active and involved in the life of the parish.

May our sharing in Holy Communion this day give us the wisdom and grace we need to be better stewards of our time and talent. By participating in the Body and Blood, Soul and Divinity of Jesus, may we have the insight and the courage to *"put the golf balls in first."*

✠ **Twenty-ninth Sunday in Ordinary Time (A)**
October 20, 2002

The Need to Give

Though it makes most Catholics uncomfortable, preaching about stewardship of treasure is essential, especially in this age of rampant consumerism. The Lord Himself never stops reminding us that sometimes material possessions are too important to us.

There is perhaps no finer Gospel passage to conclude our three week reflection on Stewardship than the words of Jesus proclaimed this morning. "Which commandment of the Law is the greatest?" the Pharisee asked. Jesus' reply: *"You shall love the Lord your God with all your heart, and with all your soul, and with all your mind."* [19]

As we have been learning, stewardship is not simply about the portion of our time, talent, and treasure that we share with the Church. *Stewardship is about all our gifts* and how we are called to be good stewards in every dimension of our lives: loving God not half-heartedly or part way, but with all our heart, mind, and soul.

These past two weeks I have spoken about *stewardship as a way of life deeply rooted in the person and teachings of Jesus Christ.* Stewardship is about being *grateful* for all of God's blessings, being *responsible* and prudent in the use of those gifts, and *sharing* those gifts

---

[19] Matthew 22:37.

generously out of a sense of love and justice. Stewardship is ultimately about **making a return** to the Lord with increase, from all that He has given.

Last weekend I spoke of the stewardship of time and talent. Today I speak of **stewardship of treasure.** I do so for several reasons:

First, because our parish and archdiocese depend upon good stewardship of treasure. This should come as no surprise to anyone!

A **second,** more important reason for speaking of stewardship of treasure is because so many people struggle with the stewardship of their personal finances:

- 49% of American families don't pay their bills on time.
- 65% don't do a good job of staying out of debt.
- 65% don't balance their checkbook.
- 82% don't adequately save for future needs.
- 50% of all marriages end in divorce, and a majority of those getting divorces point to finances as one of the primary causes of the breakup.[20]

It is not good for a family to struggle financially. It's one thing when bills pile up because of catastrophic medical or legal bills, or because of an unexpected lay-off. It's another thing when the problem is mushrooming credit card debt caused by out of control spending habits. Poor stewardship of treasure is never good for marriage and family life.

Assuming that the national statistics could also be applied to our own community, it's vital that I speak of these matters today, for some of our families may be among those who need extra encouragement to get control of their finances. If you need help in this area, please know that I can direct you to individuals in the parish who are willing to assist

---

[20] From *The Catholic Answers Guide to Family Finances,* by Philip Lenahan, Catholic Answers, 2000, p. 1.

you in developing a strategy to get out of debt and in control of your finances, providing the benefit of financial freedom and the opportunity to use your gifts of treasure for the glory and honor of God.

Third, I speak of stewardship of treasure because all of us are called to a *spirit of generosity* with our gifts of treasure. A miser is not a happy person. On the other hand we all know people who share generously of their resources, people who are usually happy and at peace with themselves. Happiness comes from sharing, from being generous, and from using one's finances for the sake of something greater than one's self, especially when that "something greater" is the up-building of the Kingdom of God.

Simply put, though we often *give to a need,* we all have a *need to give.* Even if the parish were to receive a financial windfall, I would still need to preach about Stewardship of Treasure, for we all have a need to give.

Finally, as I have been saying these past two weeks, our parish has been built, maintained, and expanded by the *generosity* of good stewards of treasure: people of faith who gave not because they had to, but because of a spirit of wanting to give back to God a portion of what He had given to them. This pattern of giving here at St. Louis Parish continues to be the way of life to which we are called.

I ask you to consider prayerfully your response to this year's Parish Stewardship and United Catholic Appeal. Consider how you have been blessed. Consider how rewarding it is to be part of the ongoing growth and vitality of our parish.

Simply balancing our budget accomplishes only part of what God is calling us to as a parish. We need to do more than that. Not reflected in our budget are the needs to:

• *Maintain a standard of excellence in our school,* in a manner that is affordable to our families. Only a part of this need is reflected in the budget. *We need to do better.*

• *Increase the number of programs for our parish families,* strengthening marriage and family life, striving to stem the tide of divorce in our community, working to build healthy, holy families. These programs are not in the budget. *We need to do better.*

• *Offer more programs that assist adults in articulating the Catholic faith* in a manner that is authentic and persuasive. There are many people in our community without a church. We must reach out to welcome them.

There are many who are going to church this Sunday elsewhere, even though they started out here at St. Louis. We all know that there are churches in town in which *our Catholic faith is attacked,* especially our doctrines concerning the Holy Eucharist, the Blessed Virgin Mary, the Sacrament of Penance, and the role of the Holy Father.

We need to be able to stand up to this opposition. When we have friends who are leaning away from our Catholic faith we need to be able to offer them reasons to come back home. Frankly, several generations of Catholics received religious instruction that lacked substance .And yet our budget contains only some funds for this purpose. *We need to do better.*

I pray that our parish will be vibrant and dynamic. I will work hard toward that end, but I need your help, your involvement and commitment. You know the difference between involvement and commitment, don't you? In the bacon and eggs that I had last Sunday morning for breakfast, the chicken was involved, the pig was committed. We need to be involved in the life of the parish and we also need to be committed!

You will receive in the mail the materials for our Parish Stewardship and United Catholic Appeal. As you prepare your intention card, please do so with three principles in mind:

Please make your gift to the Church a *planned* gift. Not haphazard, but planned. Use envelopes. When you are on vacation, mail the envelope to the parish office. Consider using automatic payments from your bank to ours. *Make your gift planned, for the Lord deserves nothing less.*

Please make your gift *proportionate.* Make your gift proportionate to the manner in which you have been blessed. What does it say if a person's gift remains the same amount through the years even when that person's income steadily rises? On the other hand what a difference it makes when a person decides to give a certain percentage of his or her income to the Lord.

Make your gift proportionate, and please consider the biblical standard of *the tithe* (ten percent). Many people (including myself) have found it helpful to give 5% of their income to the parish, 1% to the United Catholic Appeal, and 4% to charities of their choosing. *Please consider giving in a manner proportionate to how you have been blessed.* Remember that the Lord will not be outdone in generosity.

Please make your gift *sacrificial.* Give to the Lord *a gift that is meaningful to you, a gift that you are proud to present to the Lord* as a means of giving thanks for all that He has done for you.

Every person here is invited to participate in building the Kingdom of God through the stewardship of time, talent, and treasure. As we partake of the Holy Eucharist this morning, may we be conscious and grateful for all that the Lord does for us, especially in *giving us everything He has to give* through His sacrifice on the cross. Nourished by the Lord's Body and Blood, Soul and Divinity, may we be strengthened in our ability to love the Lord with all our heart, with all our mind and with all our strength.

✠ **The Thirtieth Sunday in Ordinary Time (A)**
October 27, 2002

CHAPTER TWO:
CONVERSION OF HEART

The Lord never ceases calling us to conversion of heart. One who listens carefully to the Scriptures at Mass and to the teachings of the Church will be challenged to turn toward the Lord and to follow Him without counting the cost. Let there be no doubt, this wholehearted way of following Jesus is learned over the course of the decades, rather than the years. Conversion of life is both the starting point and the effect of embracing stewardship as a way of life.

✠

Why Jesus Came

Midnight Mass of the Great Jubilee Year 2000 was a very special occasion. As we celebrated the coming of the Son of God into the world, we remembered how He charges every steward to build up the Kingdom of God.

One year ago this night Pope John Paul II opened the Holy Doors at St. Peter's in Rome, thereby ushering in the great Jubilee Year of our redemption. The worldwide celebration of the Jubilee has been memorable: the emotional visit of Pope John Paul to the Holy Land and the World Youth Day that brought millions of young people together in Rome for prayer and for celebration of our faith. Closer to home, 30,000 Catholics from throughout the Archdiocese of Indianapolis gathered in the RCA Dome for the Jubilee Mass, celebrating the outpouring of the Holy Spirit in the Sacrament of Confirmation.

In contrast to the secular celebrations of the new millennium, the Jubilee Year did not take the form of fireworks and galas. Rather, it has been the occasion for an *inner renewal of faith* and a sharing of that faith with others through the work of **evangelization.**

These two elements of the Jubilee celebration, inner renewal and evangelization, are modeled upon the person of Jesus Himself. For Jesus came to earth to do two things: *to save us* and *to charge us* as stewards with the responsibility of building up the Kingdom of God.

On this Christmas night, let me say a word about each:

Jesus came to save us. He came to rescue us from the deadly snares of sinfulness, snares from which we are unable to free ourselves. Sin separates us from God. Sin ruptures relationships. Serious sin leads us to eternal damnation, for we are all accountable for our actions.

On our own we are powerless against the wages of sin. Like a deadly microbe vulnerable only to a specific antibiotic, sin defies our own ability to resist. No one is immune to the reality of sin.

Jesus enters into our world to make a difference. Totally borne by God's grace, the Blessed Mother gave birth to the child who would take upon His own shoulders the debt of our sin, and who would ransom us from sin and death by paying the price with His own blood.

Jesus saves us by His cross. He saves us by forgiving our sins and by offering us the grace we need to live holy and morally upright lives. He is born into our world so that we might be born into His heavenly kingdom. He walks in our shoes so that we might follow Him on the road to heaven. He becomes man so that men and women might share in the life of God.

Jesus came to save us. And so the celebration of the Jubilee has emphasized the importance of our acceptance of the gift of salvation. We are invited, not forced, to accept His gift. *We are invited to accept personally the love of Jesus by embracing a lifestyle of conversion:* repenting of our sins and accepting God's grace, making possible a change of life. Jesus not only makes *a* difference. He makes *the* difference between sin and grace, damnation and salvation, death and life.

Praise God that our Jubilee celebration has seen countless numbers of people returning to the sacraments, coming to Church again and embracing Jesus as the Lord of their lives. Praise God indeed, for Jesus saves!

Having saved us, Jesus charges us with the responsibility of building up the Kingdom of God. "Go therefore and make disciples of all nations," Jesus commands his disciples, "baptizing them in the name of the Father and of the Son and of the Holy Spirit, teaching them to observe all that I have commanded you."[21] Salvation is not simply a personal matter. *Salvation draws us into the Church and into her mission of evangelization:* spreading the Gospel by word and deed. Jesus saves us not just for our own personal well-being in the afterlife, but also that through us others might know the goodness and love of God.

Praise God that our Jubilee celebration has seen countless people take a hard look at their lives and decide, with God's grace, that they need to be good stewards and to do more to reach out to others – to perform works of mercy, to share their time, talent, and treasure, to encourage others to turn to Jesus as Lord of their lives. Just as the Blessed Virgin Mary both accepted Jesus into her life and then gave Him to the world, so are we invited to find meaning and purpose in our lives by accepting Jesus and sharing Him with others through our Christian witness.

The Jubilee Year will soon be over, the banners furled, the Holy Doors closed. But God's invitation to follow Him is always open. *He will never stop inviting us to follow*

---

[21] Matthew 28:19-20a.

Him – to live a life of conversion, of renewal of spirit, of self-giving in imitation of our Master, Jesus Christ.

Each person here is called to follow the Lord Jesus in the communion of the Church. ***If you have not made clear your decision to follow Jesus with your whole heart, make that choice this holy night.*** If you are wishy-washy in your observance of the Christian life, resolve tonight to become more diligent in your faith. If you are away from the Church, not attending Mass every Sunday, let this night be the end of that. Come home, come back, return to the Church and rediscover your faith. And do it today, this holy night.

Why today? Because this is the day the Lord gives you. He gives you today, but He does not promise tomorrow. We know "neither the day nor the hour."[22]

May God bless you in abundance this holy Christmas night. May you cherish the special moments with family and friends and enjoy all of the holiday traditions. Above all, may you grow closer to Jesus, the Word of God, the Bread of Life, the King of kings and the Lord of lords. He was born for you. Please God, may you now live for Him.

✠ Christmas: The Mass at Midnight
December 25, 2000

---

[22] Matthew 25:13.

Family Virtues

The family is the domestic Church, the ideal place for the steward to grow in the virtues of gratitude, responsibility and generosity. Thank God for these important opportunities that form us and our children.

The Sunday after Christmas is the annual observance of the **Feast of the Holy Family.** We contemplate each Christmas the scene of the Blessed Mother and Saint Joseph caring for the Christ Child from the time He was an infant until He was a young man. In today's Gospel we get a glimpse of Jesus at the age of twelve.

Even if St. Luke had not divulged Our Lord's age, we could tell that He is twelve because His parents are upset with Him, and because of His response to His parents: "Did you not know that I must be in my Father's house?"[23] Only a twelve-year-old would respond so innocently, only a twelve-year-old who had learned from His parents never to be ashamed of His religious convictions.

After all, Mary and Joseph probably endured more than a few disparaging comments about the unusual circumstances surrounding the conception and birth of Jesus. Jesus learned from them what it meant to stand up for the truth no matter what anybody else was saying. He learned from them the human qualities needed to live out one's religious convictions with pride, dignity, and confidence.

You see, **the family is where children and parents alike become better stewards of God's many gifts,** for it is in the give and take of family life that we learn the virtues of which St. Paul speaks: **kindness, humility, gentleness, patience, and forgiveness.**[24]

---

[23] Luke 2:49.
[24] Cf. Colossians 3:12,13.

Let me be more specific:

Kindness: In the family we learn how to take care of others: the infant who is cranky from lack of sleep, the toddler who is afraid when Mom and Dad are out for the evening, the teenager who is devastated when cut from the basketball team. *We learn in the family how important it is to be kind to one another,* especially when the other is hurting.

Humility: Parents learn this when the kids ask questions for which there are no answers. Children learn this when they find out the hard way that there are always limits to freedom, at least while living at home. And spouses learn this at those moments when they realize that they couldn't possibly raise their kids without the constant help of a good and loving God. *We learn to be humble in the family.*

Gentleness: Is there any sight more pleasing to God than a 275-pound former linebacker holding in his arms his 6 pound, 6 ounce newborn daughter? *Gentleness is a virtue especially well-suited for gentlemen* – a virtue learned in the family.

Patience: Need I say more? Patience is learned in every household in which there are more people than bathrooms. Patience is learned when Dad is a saver and Mom is a spender, when the boys want to watch football, but the girls are watching figure skating. Patience is learned at the dinner table, where we can't eat until we've said Grace and we can't leave until everyone is finished. Without patience the world gets pretty mean and ugly. Thank God it is learned in the family.

Finally, **forgiveness.** We learn what forgiveness is all about when the milk is spilled, the vase is broken, the fender is dinged, or the curfew is missed. There may well be a time-out, restitution, or grounding, but true forgiveness is learned when no grudge is held nor is the offense mentioned again.

"I'm sorry" is so hard to say, and "I forgive you" is so easy. We learn in the family that we cannot do without either one.

It might not seem like much, but what happens in the family day in and day out is of great importance to our society and to our Church. We see so much sadness in our world because people are lacking in kindness, humility, gentleness, patience, and forgiveness. We wonder how differently some people would have turned out if they had a better opportunity to learn the virtues in the unique classroom that is the family.

What happens in the family is so very important, for *the family is the building block, the fundamental cell of our Church and our civilization.*

Three points to conclude:

1. Let us enjoy family life. It is true that life is too short, too busy, too complicated. But when our family relationships are in order life is bearable, and even a joy. This is not automatic, and sadly we sometimes fall terribly short of the goal. But we can do no better than to be our best for our family — to be present, to be engaged, to make family life a priority.

2. To be our best for our family means being as close to the Lord as possible. Taking time to pray, making Sunday Mass the fixed point of the week, and making regular use of the Sacrament of Penance is so important if we are to be the very best for our family.

3. That we might be as close to the Lord as possible, let us invoke the intercession of Saint Joseph and the Blessed Virgin Mary, those two great stewards of the Holy Family, those two great saints who intercede for us, that our families might be holy, healthy, and happy.

✠ **The Feast of the Holy Family (C)**
December 28, 2003

What About Jesus?

The Magi present their gifts before the Christ Child, the priceless gift of the Father to the human race. This Epiphany homily speaks of the good steward as one who is ever grateful for the gift of new life in Christ and who is always eager to share that gift with others.

The Feast of the Epiphany is sometimes called "Little Christmas" for in many countries this is the day that gifts are exchanged, in imitation of the wise men who brought their gifts to the Christ Child.

Epiphany means manifestation – a revelation or showing. On this day the prophecy of Isaiah was fulfilled, the prophecy that the light of the Lord would be revealed to the nations and that all people would come to proclaim the praises of the Lord.[25]

The Church keeps this feast because there is simply too much in the mystery of the Word becoming Flesh to be contained in a single day.

You see, until the birth of Jesus, God had limited His public revelation to the People of Israel, a relatively small group of people in an obscure part of the world. God did not speak in the same personal way to the Egyptians, the Greeks, the Romans, or the Persians, all of whom had built great empires and civilizations. No, during that time God focused upon the People of Israel, the descendants of Abraham and Isaac and Jacob. Instead of working with those who would be remembered for their architecture, their roads, and their conquests, God was working with a people of faith, a people who considered their greatest gifts to be His Law (the Torah) and His presence abiding in the Temple.

---

[25] Cf. Isaiah 60:1-6.

For hundreds of years the true God was unknown throughout the vast majority of the world. *All of that would change with the birth of a child.* All of that would change when, in the fullness of time, God would make His presence known by assuming the flesh and blood of our human existence. For "the Word became flesh and dwelt among us."[26]

God became man not only for the salvation of the people of Israel, but also for the salvation of all mankind. This Feast of the Epiphany reminds us that *Jesus is born so that all people might come to know the saving power of God.*

Three wise men – three kings from the ends of the earth – come to acknowledge the marvels of God in the Child Jesus. The gifts they bring point to His identity: gold is given as a gift fit for a king; frankincense is offered to honor Jesus' divinity; and the mysterious gift of myrrh[27] is presented to foreshadow the death of the Son of God. For this child is born into the world so that He might die to set us free from the power of sin and death.

Jesus Christ, honored and worshipped by the Magi, is the great light for all of humanity.

Jesus Christ, to whom the Magi brought their precious gifts, is the gift of God the Father to the whole human race.

Jesus Christ is the answer to our problems, the solution to our quest for meaning and purpose.

Jesus Christ is the sure and certain moral compass who shows us the way through the complexity and danger of this life.

Jesus Christ is the God-Man who enters into our human experience so that we might have entrance into His divinity.

---

[26] John 1:14.
[27] Myrrh is a precious resin used in burial rites.

The Feast of the Epiphany celebrates Jesus Christ as the Savior of the human race. He is the Way, the Truth, and the Life.[28]

We honor Him by our gifts – gifts of devotion, obedience, and worship. We honor Him by giving Him not just tokens of respect, but the gift of our very selves. The wise men did not bring Jesus anything but the best they had to offer. Neither should we.

The wise men returned to their homeland telling others of the wonders of the newborn King. So should we. ***Our faith is meant to be lived*** and it is meant to find expression in our inviting others to come find Him in His Church, in His Blessed Sacrament.

Once there was a young man who went away to college. After his first semester he returned home for Christmas. He was eager to tell his parents about all of the interesting people he had met and the different ways in which people view the world.

Eventually, he told his parents that he had not been going to Mass, and that he felt comfortable with this decision. There are many paths to the truth, after all, and no one religion is better than any other. It was going to be an adventure for him as he sought to learn which one of the many faith traditions represented on campus best fit his unique spiritual needs.

So his parents looked at one another, and considered his statements. Just when his father was about ready to ask, "Is this what I'm spending $25,000 a year for?" the mother quietly asked her son the question, ***"But what about Jesus?"***

It was a question for which the young man was unprepared.

---

[28] Cf. John 14:6.

Amidst his semester of ruminating about the meaning of life, he had not once thought about the person of Jesus – His teachings, His miracles, His suffering, death, and resurrection.

He had been blinded by the glare of what was new and different. His pride kept him from trusting what was tried and true. He was attracted not to lasting treasure, but to fool's gold.

"What about Jesus?" It was this question that hit the mark and that eventually drew that young man back to the sacraments.

Jesus Christ. The same yesterday, today, and forever. The Way, the Truth, and the Life. The Light to the nations. The Redeemer of the human race. And the One who cares about you and me to the point of death.

May we never abandon or take for granted the precious gift of faith in Jesus Christ. As good stewards, may we be eager to share that precious gift with others, asking gently but firmly the question that makes a difference: *"What about Jesus?"*

✠ **The Solemnity of the Epiphany of the Lord**
January 4, 2004

Come and See

Ongoing conversion of life is the task of every steward: turning away from sin to follow the Lord Jesus. The good steward responds to the challenge of the Gospel by entering more deeply into union with the Lord and communion in His Church.

What are you looking for?" Jesus directed that question to the two disciples of John the Baptist, who, in turn, had been directed by John to pay attention to the "Lamb of God" as He passed by.[29]

The Church draws our attention to this passage early in the liturgical year to remind us that from the outset of His ministry Jesus reached out and invited others to follow Him. Just as Jesus queried those two disciples, so too does He ask each of us this morning, "What are you looking for?"

We look for *material prosperity*, even though true happiness comes from spiritual riches.

We look for *security,* even though the best things in life are the surprises God has in store for us.

We look for the *understanding and closeness* of others, even though the heart remains restless until it rests in God.[30]

We look for *physical health and fitness,* even though all eternity hangs upon our spiritual well-being, the state of the soul.

We look for – long for -- good things, even though there are better things to be found in the hands of God. *"What are you looking for?" Jesus asks us.*

We might feel awkward in answering that question, for how does one articulate the soul's deepest desires? Notice that the two disciples in the Gospel don't know how to respond when Jesus asks them, "What are you looking for?" They answer His question with one of their own: "Where are you staying?"[31]

Jesus is very much at ease with their question, because it reveals to Him that they are being drawn to what is good, what is holy, what is true, what is lasting.

---

[29] Cf. John 1:35-38a.
[30] Cf. St. Augustine, *Confessiones* 1,1,1: PL 32, 659-661; quoted in CCC 30.
[31] John 1:38.

"Come and see,"[32] Jesus invites the disciples.

"Come and see where I am staying. Where I abide you will find everything your heart could ever desire, and more." "Come and see where I abide," Jesus says to each of us, "and you will find life, life in abundance."[33]

Last weekend at this Mass a number of men and women made public their heartfelt desire to follow the Lord Jesus and to enter the Church through the Sacrament of Baptism. Others with them asked for our prayers as they prepare to be received into full communion with our Catholic Church.[34]

We pray for them: that by God's grace they will persevere along the path of conversion and that they will find everything they are looking for ... and more. And we pray for ourselves: *that by God's grace we will remain attentive to the call to ongoing conversion of life.*

You see, when those two disciples decided to follow Jesus, they set out on a life characterized by the unceasing challenge of Jesus' words and example. They would be reminded repeatedly that the living of the Christian life, the life of the steward, is a task never completed here on earth; there is always more to learn, always more to put into practice in daily living.

Love your enemies, Jesus would teach.[35] Forgive your brother not seven times, but seventy times seven.[36] Take up your cross and follow in my footsteps.[37]

These are all challenges from the Lord. Challenges that keep His followers on the right path, challenges that motivate

---

[32] John 1:39.
[33] Cf. John 10:10.
[34] The Rite of Acceptance into the catechumenate took place one week earlier.
[35] Cf. Matthew 5:44.
[36] Cf. Matthew 18:22.
[37] Cf. Matthew 16:24.

the Christian steward to move from complacency into genuine attentiveness to God's will.

Come and see and **abide with me**, Jesus says.

Do not be content with simply knowing **about** Me, but **get to know Me personally** in the sacraments, especially in the Sacrament of Penance and in the *"Breaking of Bread"* [38] that is the Holy Eucharist.

Do not be content as a nominal Catholic Christian, one who fulfills the precepts of the Church, but inwardly remains unaffected by the power of the Word of God and the power of the sacraments. Rather, Jesus invites us: **Surrender yourself to the good life of abiding in My presence.** Come follow Me!

What does it mean to respond to Jesus' invitation to "Come and see"?

It means **taking time to pray** – to open one's heart to the Lord, to be truly attentive to His will. What a tremendous help the Lord gives us in our prayer by "abiding with us" in the Blessed Sacrament. What consolation one can find by making a regular commitment to spend a few moments or even an entire hour in His presence, either before the tabernacle in church or in the Perpetual Adoration Chapel. "Come and see" means growing in holiness through prayer.

"Come and see" means **embracing a life of ongoing conversion.** What in my life needs to be confessed and changed? What habits have I clung to for too long? Do I drink too much? Gamble too much? Watch television or use the internet at the expense of chastity? Do I obey the Church's teaching on pre-marital sex, contraception, adultery and coveting the flesh? Do I covet goods or forget to thank God for blessings received? Do I share my blessings generously?

---

[38] CCC 1329.

"Come and see" means *embracing a life of ongoing conversion,* rejecting the status of nominal Catholic, and allowing the Lord Jesus to form you into nothing less than a saint!

"Come and see" means *reaching out to others.* Jesus called his disciples not simply for the sake of their own salvation, but so that the Church might be established as the means of salvation for all people everywhere.

"Come and see" means sharing our gifts of time, talent, and treasure for the sake of the less fortunate and reaching out to those who have no church to call their own. This is what we mean by the terms *stewardship* and *evangelization.* Both are matters of the heart. Both are matters that call us to action and to increased involvement in the life of the Church.

As we prepare to renew our commitment to the Lord Jesus through the Sacrament of the Eucharist, may our hearts always remember the Lord's penetrating question and His open-hearted invitation:

"What are you looking for?" *"Come and see."*

✠ **The Second Sunday in Ordinary Time (B)**
January 16, 2000

The Call of Simon

Some in our Church are called to follow the Lord as priests or consecrated religious. The message of stewardship encourages our youth to ask the question, "What, dear Lord, do you want me to do to fulfill Your will for the Church?"

Every time I celebrate the Eucharist I make it a practice to pray silently for those young men whom I know to be considering or preparing for ordination to the priesthood. I pray as well for those men and women who are discerning the call to the religious life. I pray for them by name during the quiet time after the distribution of Holy Communion.

Many of the young people on my list **enjoy the support of their families as they pursue their vocation.** Sadly, others do not. Their families actively discourage them. "Is a religious vocation a good thing or a bad thing?" they ask. "Can a person ever be happy as a priest or a sister?" "How can anyone give up marriage, children and grandchildren?" "It seems like such a waste."

If this is said today, I suspect that it was said 2000 years ago on the shore of the Sea of Galilee. Simon was doing well for himself. Recent excavations have uncovered his house, which was larger than many in Capernaum. He was a small business owner: he had one boat, maybe more; he had James and John as his business partners, and most likely had hired hands in his employ. To top it off, Simon was a fisherman! He made his living on one of the most beautiful and bountiful lakes in the world. What a life!

And then Simon met Jesus. Was that a good thing or a bad thing?

As a result of that meeting Simon abandoned his boats and his nets. He left everything behind. No longer did Simon work for himself; now he was a follower of an itinerant preacher. No longer did Simon call all the shots; now he had to get along with eleven other apostles. No longer did Simon work amidst the beauty of the Sea of Galilee; now he was on the road, withstanding the rigors of travel along dusty roads and in noisy cities. No longer was Simon working in the straightforward business of fishing; now he was in the middle of complex theological debates and convoluted disputes over religious practice.

Just a few years later Simon would leave his home country, never to see it again. He would go to Rome where he would be arrested for his religious beliefs, be convicted of treason, and be crucified upside down in the circus of Nero for the amusement of the Roman emperor.

Simon met Jesus on the shore of the Sea of Galilee. Was that a good thing or a bad thing? Was Simon Peter's life well-lived or a waste of time?

There are two measures of a person's life: the standards of the world on one hand and the criterion of faith in Jesus Christ on the other.

We know all too well **the standards of this world.** They are presented to us on television, in the secular press, and in the fashion of the day. We are bombarded with a clear and consistent message about how to find happiness, what is acceptable behavior, and who is important in our society. We are saturated from infancy with the doctrines of this world: money and power bring happiness; morality is relative; human life is precious not all of the time, but only some of the time.

Faith in Jesus Christ asserts another way, "a still more excellent way,"[39] in the words of St. Paul. Happiness comes not from one's possessions, but through a life of loving service. Right can be distinguished from wrong, and the Ten Commandments tell us how. Discipline, character, and responsibility are to be honored and praised. Every human life is sacred, from the moment of conception until the hour of natural death.

The Christian way doesn't make sense in our world, yet it is our world's only hope to stop the spiraling descent into self-destruction.

---

[39] I Corinthians 12:31.

The Christian steward knows this and lives his or her life so as to give hope to those caught up in the darkness of the ways of the world. The good steward is "the light of the world,"[40] illuminating the path so that others might recognize the Way, the Truth, and the Life who is Jesus Christ.[41]

To be hope for the world one must know Jesus. If we don't know Jesus, we are of no use to anyone. And we get to know Jesus through the repentance of our sins and through knowledge of His Word in Scripture and Church teaching. We deepen that knowledge by participation in the Sacraments, especially Penance and the Holy Eucharist, the life-blood of His Holy Church.

Simon Peter wanted to know Jesus, and so he followed Him. Not always perfectly, mind you, but he followed the Lord ***faithfully.***

Those who aspire to the priesthood and religious life want to know Jesus as well, and we must pray that they will always stay close to Jesus and find in Him the consolation that comes from following Him, the peace that this world cannot give.[42] Each one here, every member of the Church, is invited, encouraged, and urged to ***know the Lord Jesus: personally, intimately, as a true friend.***

Stewards are called to know Jesus and to follow Him. Following Jesus means leaving certain worldly attractions behind, leaving our boats and nets by the shore, as it were. It means making clear choices, especially the choice to turn away from sin. Let's each pray for the grace to do that wisely and humbly.

To know Jesus, to follow Jesus, and to persevere through the years until we wear the crown of victory – this

---

[40] Matthew 5:14.
[41] Cf. John 14:6.
[42] Cf. John 14:27.

is our calling, and this is the greatest mark we can leave upon this troubled world of ours. A bad thing? A waste of time? I think not. Not for Simon Peter. Not for priests and religious. Not for any follower of Jesus.

⊠ The Fifth Sunday in Ordinary Time (C)
February 4, 2001

Change Your Ways!

The season of Lent is "spring training" for the steward: a graced time for clarifying one's priorities in life and recommitting one's self to the task of following the Lord unreservedly.

The word **Lent** is derived from an Old English word that means **springtime.** And springtime, thank God, is a time of change. Between now and Easter we will witness a beautiful change, a **profound transformation** in nature from death to life, from hibernation to activity, from barrenness to fertility.

And as nature around us changes during Lent, so must we. **The season of Lent provides us an opportunity to commence with that change.** We pray more intensely, thereby drawing closer to the Lord. We commit to fasting, thereby distancing ourselves from those attachments that get in the way of our holiness and well-being.

Sin has been defined as an undue attachment to the things of this world. Isn't that the truth! Not that the things of this world are bad in and of themselves, for they are not. For everything there is a time and a purpose. But **undue** attachment to the things of the world is rightly called sinful.

Whether those things of this world are food or drink, possessions, sensuality, or power, our undue attachment to them is always our undoing. Of those undue attachments we must repent and from them we must turn.

St. Paul speaks about the importance of changing our ways. In fact, he addresses strong words to his readers. He says that for some, their God is their belly and their glory is in their shame.[43] (How's that for tact!) In other words their God, their number one priority in life, is self-fulfillment, the satisfaction of carnal urges, and sensory pleasure.

That's how those other people are, St. Paul says, those citizens of the world who don't know any better, who never learned right from wrong, and whose "minds [are] set on earthly things".[44] That's how those other people are, St. Paul says, but good stewards are different.

We are not like other people. ***Our citizenship is in heaven***,[45] St. Paul reminds us. We belong to a different order of things because we know Jesus and we are members of His Body, the Church. We are not like the other people who don't know any better. ***We know who we are.*** We know who redeemed us and at what considerable cost our ransom was paid. And we act like citizens of heaven – or at least we try to.

A young man was going away to fulfill his military obligation. His family, of course, was nervous about his departure, knowing that his time in the service would take him a long way from home and expose him to many temptations and to situations that could distract him from his Christian responsibilities. His grandmother called him aside before he left for boot camp, and she said to him with conviction, "Just remember who you are and how you were

---

[43] Cf. Philippians 3:19.
[44] Philippians 3:19.
[45] Cf. Philippians 3:20.

raised. Remember to go to church every Sunday and to pray every day." The young man would later say that even given all the commands directed to him by his drill instructor, it was the words of his grandmother that would resonate in his mind and in his heart for the rest of his life. "Remember who you are and how you were raised."

The life of the steward is that simple. The world presents many things to us that are attractive to the senses but deadly to the soul. *We must always remember who we are.* In times of temptation we must remember that we *do* know better than others who do not share our moral convictions. Just because it is popular or accepted does not make it right. We know better. We were raised to know better. We are not like other people for our citizenship is in heaven. *If it feels from time to time that our morals are out of place in this world, it's because they are.* We are in exile, as it were, from our homeland. There is a kingdom of this world and a kingdom of heaven. May we never forget in which kingdom we have our citizenship.

In today's Gospel reading, Jesus takes his closest disciples atop Mount Tabor and teaches them a lesson about change.[46] In fact His body is transfigured (changed) right before their eyes. Jesus reveals to His apostles His divinity, and in so doing He shows them the possibility of change in their humanity. Just as Jesus was transfigured, so too would Peter, James, and John experience profound change for the better in their own lives here on earth. They would participate in His glory in heaven.

And so, too, for us. *We need to change,* so let's do it. Let's do it this Lent. It's a grace to recognize that we need to change – and to realize that we can't change on our own. *We need Jesus.* We need His grace and His strength, both of which we find in abundance in the sacraments of the Church.

---

[46] Cf. Luke 9: 28b-36.

The grace that comes from making a good, honest confession is what makes it possible for good intentions to be transfigured into practical, concrete, real life choices. The grace of the Sacrament of Penance frees us from our undue attachment to the things of this world. ***The substantial presence of Jesus in the Sacrament of the Holy Eucharist gives us the ability to remember who we are***, to remember that we are citizens of a kingdom not of this world, and to persevere in the fundamental decisions we make to follow the Lord and to follow Him unreservedly.

There is a kingdom of this world and a kingdom of heaven. ***May we never forget*** in which kingdom we have our citizenship.

✠ **The Second Sunday of Lent (C)**
March 7, 2004

The Good Shepherd

The tragic events at Columbine High School in 1999 took place the week before this homily for Good Shepherd Sunday. Because stewardship is counter-cultural, the steward knows how seductive can be the influence of the Evil One, and strives to remain always within range of the voice of the Good Shepherd.

The scriptures proclaim consistently and clearly our need for Jesus, the Good Shepherd. The First Reading tells us of Peter's great Pentecost sermon in Jerusalem: "Repent, and be baptized into Jesus Christ," St. Peter urges. "Save yourselves from this corrupt generation."[47] St. Peter's

---

[47] Cf. Acts 2:38,40.

distinction between the corruption of this generation on one hand, and salvation in Jesus Christ on the other is echoed in the Second Reading, where he reminds us that once we had all gone astray like sheep. Now, *by the grace of God and the power of the cross of Jesus, we have "returned to the Shepherd and Guardian of [our] souls."* [48]

Our Church teaches that throughout the history of all peoples and in the life of each person *there is waged a "dramatic [struggle] between good and evil, between light and darkness."* [49] Each of us hears competing voices: the voice of the Good Shepherd, who knows His sheep and calls each one by name, opposed by the voice of the stranger, the thief, the one who employs every deception to lure the sheep out of the safety of the sheepfold.

The Good Shepherd seeks only the welfare of the sheep – to lead them to verdant pastures and restful waters – that they might produce good wool year after year. The Good Shepherd comes that the sheep *"may have life and have it abundantly."* [50] In deadly contrast, the *"thief comes only to steal and kill and destroy."* [51]

This struggle between good and evil, light and darkness was played out in dramatic fashion this past Tuesday afternoon in Littleton, Colorado. We see clearly the corrosive consequences of attentiveness to the deceptions of the thief, the Evil One. Somehow those two boys at Columbine High School got on the wrong track. By the things they read, listened to, or talked about, their souls were corrupted to such an extent that they engaged in a kind of terror that seems to bear the authorship of Satan himself. "For the thief comes only to steal and kill and destroy." [52]

---

[48] 1 Peter 2:25.
[49] *Gaudium et spes* 13 § 2.
[50] John 10:10.
[51] Ibid.
[52] Ibid.

Yet in the same incident we also witnessed shining examples of bravery, heroism and faith. Made visible to the whole world were the *inner, God-centered lives* of many students, parents, and faculty members as they came together in the aftermath of tragedy. They prayed, expressing their sorrow and their hope, sharing their need to be strong and to turn away from future violence. Members of that community continue to manifest their faith, their personal relationship with the Shepherd, the One who comes "that they may have life and have it abundantly."[53]

What happened at Columbine High this week was dramatic, intense, and specific. But the dynamics of the struggle between good and evil, light and darkness are felt universally, everyday by everyone. Every day each of us hears the voice of the Shepherd, calling us to remain within the sound of His voice, urging us to stay on the path that leads to heaven. And every day we hear the voice of the thief, the Evil One, who murmurs over and over again: "That sin isn't so bad." "You don't need to pray today." "Even though that action breaks a commandment it really doesn't matter."

Day in and day out the voice of the Shepherd and the voice of the Evil One vie for our attention. Our free will gives us the capacity to choose between the two. By our own free will we can and sometimes do follow the tempting voice of the thief who cares nothing for our temporal or eternal well being, but who comes only to destroy. For although we desire the good, the effects of original sin make us "inclined to evil and subject to error."[54] Praise God, however, that *the Good Shepherd battles the thief and fights valiantly on our behalf.* We need only to cooperate with His grace and to surrender to Him as our Champion, our Savior, and our

---

[53] Ibid.
[54] CCC 1707.

Lord. He comes that we may have life and have it to the full.[55]

We know of many distractions in our lives that feed into our human weakness and lead us into the corruption of sin. We also know that we are most likely to stay on the right path when we surround ourselves with that which is holy and honorable, noble and true.[56] **The Church provides us with tried and true ways to stay alert and responsive to the guidance of the Good Shepherd:** read the Scriptures; come to church; receive the Sacraments of Penance and the Eucharist; implore the intercession of the Blessed Mother and all the saints in heaven; live with a serious commitment to good stewardship and Christian charity; pray regularly. *If we stay close to Him, we have nothing to fear.* We will experience true happiness both on earth and in the life to come.

As we reflect upon the events of this past week in Littleton, let us remember that the tragedy provides us with a glimpse into the great battle between good and evil that is waged every day.

Denver Archbishop Charles Chaput writes the following:

"The causes of this violence are many and complicated: racism, fear, selfishness. But in another, deeper sense, the cause is very simple: *We're losing God, and in losing Him, we're losing ourselves.* The complete contempt for human life shown by the young killers at Columbine is not an accident, or an anomaly, or a freak flaw in our social fabric. It's what we create when we live a contradiction. We can't systematically kill the unborn, the infirm and the condemned prisoners among us; we can't glorify brutality in our entertainment; we can't market avarice and greed ... and then

---

[55] Cf. John 10:10.
[56] Cf. Philippians 4:8.

hope that somehow our children will help build a culture of life.

"We need to change. But societies only change when families change, and families only change when individuals change. Without a conversion to humility, non-violence, and selflessness in our own hearts, all our talk about 'ending the violence' may end as pious generalities. It is not enough to speak about reforming our society and community. We need to reform ourselves."[57]

May our sharing in the Eucharist today help us to change. May the grace of this sacrament help us to overcome temptation and keep us attuned to the voice of the Good Shepherd.

❈ **The Fourth Sunday of Easter (A)**
   April 25, 1999

Our Citizenship is in Heaven

The good steward is never quite at home in this life, because he or she senses its impermanence, for everything is a gift of God, to be given back to Him. The steward is in the world, but not of it. "Our citizenship is in heaven," says St. Paul,[58] and that means that as stewards we must always keep our eyes fixed on a farther goal, our salvation. This homily was delivered on the Solemnity of the Ascension.

Several years ago good friends of mine lost their four-year-old child. The child was born with a host of health problems and was in and out of the hospital many times

---

[57] *Denver Catholic Register,* April 28, 1999.
[58] Cf. Philippians 3:20.

before succumbing to his condition. Needless to say, the parents were devastated. No parent should ever have to bury a child, especially a child so young, so innocent.

Amidst their grief they told me that two things gave them great consolation. First, their faith told them that their son was in heaven, for he had been baptized and died with no personal sin on his soul. Second was their insight that part of them was now in heaven. Their own flesh and blood, their precious gift from God, was now in heaven, waiting for them to get there.

The parents tell me that not a day goes by that they do not think of that. Not a day goes by that they are not conscious of their calling to stay on the path that leads to heaven so that the hope of that happy reunion might one day be realized. Because of their faith and hope, they have a certain perspective on life that carries them through some days that are still very dark.

On this day when we recall the Ascension of our Lord Jesus into heaven, this day when we profess solemnly our belief that Jesus Christ ascended body and soul into heaven, we are reminded that *the good steward has a certain perspective on life,* a specific outlook on our troubled world.

You see, His body is now in heaven. The tomb is empty. He has been raised, He has ascended into heaven and now sits at the right hand of the Father. His glorified body is now in heaven. And *we are members of His body.* We are part of the Body of Christ through our Baptism into His death and resurrection and by our sharing in the Holy Eucharist. Jesus Christ is Head of the Body of Christ, and we are members of that Body. *Just like the parents of the child who died, we can say that part of us is already in heaven.* All we must do is to stay connected to Jesus Christ and we, too, will one day be with Him in heaven. Like the branches and the vine, so are we connected to our Lord Jesus, the same Lord Jesus who is seated at the right hand of the Father.

Three scripture passages come to mind in this regard:

First, "Our citizenship is in heaven."[59] St. Paul tells us that as members of Christ's body we belong in heaven, and so we will, during our time on earth, feel like foreigners, sojourners, aliens. We won't fit into the ways of this world. Our Christian faith will demand that we stand in opposition to our contemporary culture. **We are in exile from our homeland and because of that we won't fit in.** Our values will be different from those of the contemporary culture. Our morality will have higher standards. For example, even though it is legal in all fifty states and in most countries around the world, we will continue to assert that direct abortion is always morally wrong. Even though it is as common as can be, we will always maintain that co-habitation is always sinful. And though it is glorified in nearly every television show and movie produced these days, we will not back down from our stance that extramarital sexual relations can never be justified.

Our ways will seem alien to the world around us. And that is okay. That's the way it should be. For our citizenship is in heaven. We are not beholden to this world.

The second scripture quote that comes to mind is *"Here we have no lasting city."*[60] The things of this world will all pass away. Our health, our possessions, our influence – everything we have that means so much to us will one day be no more. Everything, that is, save only our eternal souls, created by God for immortality. Our flesh will one day die and decay, but our soul will live on forever, in happiness, we pray. **But we know that the decisions we make today**

---

[59] Cf. Philippians 3:20.
[60] Hebrews 13:14.

have eternal consequences. There is a heaven, and there is a less pleasant alternative. Hell is real and exists for those who persist in mortal sin.

"Here we have no lasting city." Which begs the question: Where are our priorities? Are we as concerned about the state of our immortal soul as we are about our appearance, our material prosperity, our hobbies and sports? We work hard on those things, and rightly so, but are we with equal or greater intensity "working out our salvation"[61] and helping our family and friends to make progress on the road to heaven? In the end it will matter nothing at all how much money we have in the bank. The faithful steward knows that what will matter are the spiritual treasures stored up in heaven for "Here we have no lasting city."

A final scripture quote to consider is *"Do not be conformed to this world but be transformed by the renewal of your mind."* [62] We are more than half-way to heaven, thanks be to God, for our Savior has blazed the trail before us and has opened wide the gates. But we still have far to go, and we will never make it to heaven if we are conformed to this world. If our goal in life is to be worldly, then we will never be heavenly. If our goal is to fit in to our contemporary culture, our contemporary morality, our contemporary standards, then we will never make it to heaven. If our goal is just to measure up to earthly standards, we will never find ourselves being judged worthy of heaven. "Be not conformed to this world, but be transformed by the renewal of your mind."

On this day when we remember the Ascension of our Lord into heaven, may we be even more conscious that where He has gone we hope to follow. Please God may we never lose sight of that goal. May our sharing in the Holy Eucharist be for us today *a foretaste of the heavenly*

---

[61] Cf. Philippians 2:12.
[62] Romans 12:2.

banquet. May our actions and attitudes here on earth be directed solely toward our faith's goal, our salvation. For part of us is already in heaven.

✠ **The Solemnity of the Ascension of the Lord**
June 1, 2003

Like Sheep without a Shepherd

Conversion of heart means living the good life, remaining close to the Shepherd of our souls. The steward is always grateful for the ministry of the Good Shepherd for without Him we are lost. Finding us and leading us is a tremendous gift of the Good Shepherd, the gift of salvation. So good is the Lord that He never grows weary of the task of shepherding.

H e saw a great throng, and He had compassion on them, because they were *like sheep without a shepherd.*"[63]

You know, Jesus knew a lot about sheep and shepherding. In His day everyone knew just how much sheep depended upon their shepherd. Back then the sheep were not kept in pens or behind fences. Instead, the shepherd led them cross-country from place to place. He knew the fields where the sheep could graze and find the water they needed in order to stay alive, to grow and to produce wool in abundance.

So what happens to the sheep when they are without a shepherd? Three things, to be specific:

First, they get lost! Sheep have very short attention spans and absolutely no sense of direction. Without a

---

[63] Mark 6:34, emphasis added.

shepherd to guide them, they have no chance of finding food or water, let alone making it back home to where they belong.

The second thing that happens when sheep are left without the shepherd is that *they go hungry.* You see, sheep that are skittish or nervous will not eat. The presence of the shepherd ensures that the sheep will be tranquil enough to graze to their hearts' content. But if they are without their shepherd the sheep will not be able to eat and will not survive.

Finally, sheep without shepherds get eaten by wolves. Remember the rod and the staff that give comfort to the sheep?[64] The staff is the crook that the shepherd uses to rescue the sheep from the briars. The rod is a club whose grip has been carved to match the shepherd's hand. Young shepherds practiced throwing the club until they could hit moving targets with deadly accuracy. The shepherd stands guard over his flock as the wolves circle their intended prey. When needed, the shepherd uses his rod to keep those wolves at bay. Without the shepherd, the sheep are eaten by wolves.

Jesus is the Good Shepherd. He is the one who keeps us poor sheep from getting lost. He is the one who makes sure we do not go hungry, but nourishes us well with His Body and Blood. Jesus is the one who keeps the wolves at bay – the demons that seek only to steal and slaughter and destroy.[65]

Jesus is the Good Shepherd. And *He establishes His Catholic Church as the means by which He continues to shepherd His flock.*

So that we might not get lost, Jesus teaches us how to live. The teachings of Jesus and the inspired teachings of His

---

[64] Cf. Psalm 23:4.
[65] Cf. John 10:10.

Church provide us with a reliable guide that keeps us on the right path. The term "moral compass" aptly describes the teachings of our Church. If we keep our eyes on that moral compass and trust in its reliability we will not lose our way to heaven. If we heed the teachings of the Church, especially the teachings about the dignity of the human person and the proper respect due to human sexuality, we will not wander far from the path. If we keep the commandments and draw near to the Lord through the sacraments, we will follow a guide more reliable than the North Star. We will follow the Good Shepherd.

So that we might never go hungry, Jesus gives Himself to us: Body and Blood, Soul and Divinity. Jesus bids us to eat of the Bread of Life and to drink the cup of eternal salvation. "I am the Bread of Life," Jesus says, "he who comes to me shall not hunger, and he who believes in me shall never thirst."[66] Our Shepherd is so good that He gives us this great gift at the price of His own Body and Blood.

He feeds us with His flesh and blood and bids us to eat and drink so that we might never again hunger or thirst. This is the Good Shepherd that every faithful steward knows and loves. This is Jesus, our Good Shepherd.

So that we might not be eaten by wolves, so that we might not fall victim to that which can truly harm us, the Good Shepherd stands ready to do battle with the Enemy. He fights on our behalf whenever we have the good sense to call upon His Holy Name. The devil prowls about and seeks the ruin of souls. The Great Deceiver will use every trick in the book to distract us from our Christian responsibilities and to lead us into temptation. The powers of the devil are great, but they are limited.

The Lord Jesus, the Good and gentle Shepherd, is *all-*powerful. And so when we are tempted, when we are drawn

---

[66] John 6:35.

to stray from what we know is right, when the devil seems to get the best of us, we can do no better than to call upon the Name of Jesus, the One who is always there ready to champion our cause. We take legitimate solace in His promise to be with us always, even until the end of the age.[67] His mercies are never exhausted, His favors are never spent.[68] Such is the Good Shepherd.

Sheep without a shepherd will get lost. They will go hungry. They will be eaten by wolves. *Praise God that we have so great a Shepherd,* one who will never leave His flock untended, one who lays down His life for His flock[69] so that they – so that we – might have life and have it to the full.

✠ **The Sixteenth Sunday in Ordinary Time (B)**
July 20, 2003

You Are Not an Animal

Stewardship begins in one's youth, when the good habits of self-giving, generosity, and responsibility are being formed. Contrary to popular opinion, our young people are not "animals." They are loved by the Lord who never stops calling them to the good life.

For the most part, Jesus ministered to His own people, the people of Israel. Only occasionally did He minister to the Gentiles, those who were not Jewish. Today's Gospel describes such an occasion.[70]

When Jesus ministers to this woman of the region of Tyre and Sidon, He anticipates the objections of His apostles: "It

---

[67] Cf. Matthew 28:20.
[68] Cf. Lamentations 3:22.
[69] Cf. John 10:11.
[70] Matthew 15: 21-28.

is not fair to take the children's bread and throw it to the dogs."[71] You see, many of the Jewish people of Jesus' day spoke with great contempt for the Gentiles. They were called swine or dogs, animals certainly not deserving of the dignity that is due to human beings.

It seems that down through the ages this has been our unfortunate legacy: to regard those people different from ourselves as being less than deserving of human dignity. It is how slave holders of the South regarded people of color. It is how the Nazis regarded the Jews. It is how some Israelis and some Palestinians regard each other. It is how some regard an undesired child in the womb -- as an animal, or even less than an animal, undeserving of the rights and respect that is due every human person.

Every human person is created in the image and likeness of God,[72] *created with an eternal soul, created with the capacity to know, love, and serve God.*

Jesus recognizes the dignity of the woman whom He encounters in today's Gospel. He uses the occasion to teach His disciples and to teach us that *no human being is ever outside the care and mercy of God,* no human being is ever to be treated as less than a child of God.

And yet, this is what we do. We must remind others and even ourselves of our God-given dignity. Unfortunately, I hear frequently just the opposite in regard to our young people. Yes, *our* young people, even the ones sitting among us today. "Animals," they are sometimes considered. (Perhaps some parents are thinking of their teenagers' rooms right now and are nodding their heads in total agreement!) But that laid aside, what I hear said of our young people is that they are incapable of controlling themselves and making

---

[71] Matthew 15:26.
[72] Cf. Genesis 1:26,27.

sound moral decisions in regard to the Sixth and Ninth Commandments.[73]

Some parents believe this of their own children, so much so that they arm their teenagers with pills, shots, and devices to spare them of the consequences of their lack of control. They fail to consider that there's not a device or pill in the world that can spare a young person from a broken heart or the shame of sexual exploitation. "They are just not able to control their hormones," it is said. "They are slaves to their passions."

What an awful thing to say of our young people, *to contend that they are incapable of making morally sound judgments,* that they are just like animals in heat.

Turn on the television, especially to MTV, and this is exactly what is being said. Our young people are being encouraged to: "Give in to your hormones. You can't control them anyway, so you might as well enjoy the wild life. You might as well live like 'wildlife' during your teens and early twenties. Party like an animal."

What a shame. The young people I know are capable of so much more than that. The young people I know are sharpening their minds by taking difficult classes in school. They are improving their self-control by disciplining their bodies in sports. They are showing great responsibility in their jobs and are helping out at home. They are good stewards. *They are opening their hearts to God and to our Church* and listening with rapt attention to our 82 year-old Holy Father, who has an amazing ability to connect with

---

[73] You shall not commit adultery. You shall not covet your neighbor's wife.

young people, in spite of his advancing years and physical limitations.[74]

Our young people are not animals. They are human beings who possess eternal souls and who are **capable of exercising their free will to choose what is good and noble and holy and true.**[75] They have recourse to the sacraments of the Church, especially the Holy Eucharist, to strengthen them in body, mind, and soul. They have recourse to the Sacrament of Penance, a sacrament in which a person finds forgiveness of sins and the grace of God that is necessary to make progress in the virtues and to improve one's ability to make good moral decisions.

Animals? Out of control? Slaves to their passions? To be certain, some of our young people act as if that were the case. In fact, some who are old enough to know better act as if that were the case as well. But a person who considers our young people to be animals has things very, very wrong. Each of us has been redeemed by the blood of the Lord. **Each of us is considered so dear to the Lord Jesus that He would die to accomplish our redemption,** the forgiveness of our sins. Each of us is connected to the Lord Jesus in a profound and irrevocable way,[76] so much so that **the Lord's grace makes it possible for us to rise above our human weakness and limitations and to live honorably, as children of the light.**[77]

Young people, (and others), you know the commandments. You know the consequences of sin. You know that sin is a path that you don't want to follow. Others may tell you that you cannot resist the urge to sin. I tell you

---

[74] In this homily written in August 2002, I refer to Pope John Paul II, who died on April 2, 2005, just prior to the publication of this manuscript.

[75] Cf. Philippians 4:8.

[76] Cf. Romans 11:29.

[77] Cf. Ephesians 5:8; 1 Thessalonians 5:5; 1 John 1:5-7.

that I believe in you. You are capable of so much good. ***Stay close to Jesus, stay close to the sacraments***, and you will find the grace you need to stay on the path that leads to heaven. "Resist the devil and he will flee from you. Draw near to God and he will draw near to you."[78] You are not animals. You are children of God.

✠ **The Twentieth Sunday in Ordinary Time (A)**
   August 18, 2002

The Holy Sacrifice of the Mass: Drawing Near to Calvary

The good steward stands at the foot of the cross of Jesus in awe and wonder at the Lord's sacrificial gift of Himself. On the Feast of Christ the King the steward is reminded of the responsibility of following in the footsteps of the Master.

A great treasure of our Catholic Faith is the keeping of the liturgical year. Beginning with the first Sunday of Advent, we retrace annually the key moments in the history of our redemption.

During Advent we experience the longing for the Messiah. ***At Christmas*** we celebrate the coming of our Lord. ***Through Lent and Holy Week*** we are purified and prepared for the solemn remembrance of the suffering, death and resurrection of the Lord. ***In Eastertide and Pentecost*** we are drawn more deeply into the joy of the resurrection and the coming of the Holy Spirit. And finally, ***throughout Ordinary Time*** we express our longing for the coming of

---

[78] James 4:7,8.

the Kingdom and pray for perseverance in the life of holiness and virtue.

Today, the liturgical year brings us to its last Sunday, the Feast of Christ the King. As the year draws to an end, we remember that *one day time itself will cease and the Lord Jesus Christ will come in glory* to reveal to all humanity His Kingship. In the words of the Creed, "He will come again in glory to judge the living and the dead, and His Kingdom with have no end."

Our scripture readings speak of the Kingship of Jesus. The first reading features David, in whose lineage Jesus was born – David, who was both shepherd and king and who prefigures Jesus, the Good Shepherd and the eternal King.[79] The second reading features an ancient hymn of the Church, in which Jesus is spoken of as the King of Creation, in whom all things in heaven and earth were created, and who establishes here on earth a kingdom of justice, forgiveness and peace.[80]

But it is the gospel reading[81] that gives us the greatest pause this morning. For the Gospel takes us to a place we might rather not go on our own. The Gospel on this Feast of Christ the King *takes us to Calvary,* to the foot of the cross, where we behold our King wearing a crown not of gold, but of thorns. Our Lord establishes His Kingdom neither by military conquest nor by political maneuver, but by laying down His life for the sake of the ones He loves, and even for those who "knew not what they were doing."[82]

We need to go to Calvary this day – even if we don't want to go there. I remember earlier this year when Mel

---

[79] Cf. 2 Samuel 5:1-3
[80] Cf. Colossians 1:12-20.
[81] Luke 23:35-43.
[82] Cf. Luke 23:34.

Gibson's *The Passion of the Christ* was released.[83] I can't say that I wanted to go to that movie in the way I might want to go to see the latest action or adventure movie. Nor once inside the theater did I want to watch the terrifying scene of the scourging at the pillar.

But I knew that I had to go. And I had to watch. I couldn't close my eyes and pretend that it didn't happen that way. For what was being depicted on the screen in all of its brutal cruelly was what Jesus went through so that I might enter into His life here on earth and into the joys of heaven in the hereafter.

Just as I didn't want to go to see that movie, nor do I particularly want to think too much about the details of all that Jesus endured on that Friday we call "Good". But I must do so on a regular basis lest I forget exactly who Jesus is, and precisely what He did for me – and for all of us.

That is why at the end of the liturgical year the Church would have us stand once again at the foot of the cross of Jesus. At the foot of the cross, as we look up at the figure of the Lord, wracked with pain, His every breath an agony, each one of us must ask, "Is this my King? Is this the one to whom I owe my life, my fortune, and my sacred honor?" Because *if He is our King, our lives had better bear faithful witness to His Kingship.*

Our lives ought to be lived according to high moral standards: lives of virtue, lives of dedication and devotion, lives of faithful stewardship. He died for us. He gave everything He had to give for us. He suffered unmentionable horrors for us. How then, must we live? *How do stewards of so great a King live out their lives?* How else but wholeheartedly, unreservedly, with no strings attached.

---

[83] The film was released on Ash Wednesday, 2004.

The cross of Jesus was flanked by two other crosses that day. The two other crosses represent the only two logical responses to what Jesus went through. One response was the mockery and scorn of the one who thought Jesus' death was in vain. "You saved others, why not save yourself?"[84] That is the very same response of which we are guilty every time we act as though the cross of Jesus doesn't matter. *Every time we sin*, we are the thief who mocks the sufferings of our Lord.

But there is another response, the response of Dismas, the good thief, who recognizes his own wrongdoing, his own sinfulness, and cries out for the Lord's mercy and forgiveness. "Jesus, remember me when you come in your kingly power,"[85] he implores. And when we do the same, *when we ask for mercy and pardon* from the King of Heaven and Earth, we are certain to receive what Dismas obtained: the assurance that the joy and peace of paradise is ours.

As we draw near to Calvary this day through the offering of the Holy Sacrifice of the Mass, may we be conscious of the fact that we approach the King of all Creation. Nourished with His Body and Blood, may we persevere in living our lives as loyal stewards of so great a King.

✠ **The Solemnity of Our Lord Jesus Christ the King (C)**
November 21, 2004

---

[84] Cf. Luke 23:39.
[85] Luke 23:42.

CHAPTER THREE:
COMMUNION IN
THE BODY OF CHRIST

Promoting stewardship as a way of life is a sure means of strengthening the bonds of communion with both the local and universal Church, for the Lord calls us to follow Him in the context of the Church. When a person knows Jesus, the person will also know His Bride, the Church. Stewardship is at the service of the Holy Eucharist, the means by which the Church is made one, united in communion in the Body of Christ.

✠

Why Catholics Honor Mary

A good steward need look no farther for a role model than the Blessed Virgin Mary, the first Christian steward. The long history of devotion to the Blessed Mother bears witness to the beautiful way in which she served as God's faithful steward.

On the Fourth Sunday of Advent each year the Scriptures draw our attention to the young woman from Nazareth named Mary.[86] Today's account of the Visitation of the Virgin Mary to her kinswoman Elizabeth is but one of a number of places in the Gospels where Mary is mentioned. ***Each Scriptural account of Mary is always in connection with Jesus*** at the most significant moments of His life: the Annunciation, the Nativity, His first miracle at Cana, His crucifixion.

Mary was with Jesus every step of the way, most notably today, on the occasion of Jesus' first meeting with his cousin,

---

[86] Luke 1:39-45.

John the Baptist. Though both Jesus and John were still in their mothers' wombs, the encounter was significant, for when Elizabeth heard Mary's greeting, the infant leaped in her womb, and Elizabeth cried out in a loud voice, *"Blessed are you among women, and blessed is the fruit of your womb!"* [87]

A young man whose parents emigrated from Mexico entered college this past August. The crucifix around his neck and his Hispanic surname made him an obvious target for those on campus who sought to convince him that his Catholic faith would lead him to eternal damnation. "You are not a Christian," he was told, "because Catholics are idolaters, worshipping Mary as a goddess. You need to renounce your Catholic faith and be baptized a Christian if you truly want to follow Jesus and get to heaven."

Tony's faith was strong, but he was disappointed in himself that he didn't have an articulate response to give to those who challenged his faith. Later that day, at the prompting of his Catholic roommate, Tony logged on to the *Catholic Answers* web site.[88] There he found good responses to a number of challenges to his Catholic faith, helping him to put into words what he knew in his heart to be true.

Tony knew, for example, that **we Catholics do not worship Mary, for worship is due to God alone:** Father, Son, and Holy Spirit. He learned that the word for the great respect that we show for the Blessed Mother is "veneration",[89] and Tony learned that we show the Blessed Mother the highest respect and honor for several reasons:

---

[87] Luke 1:42; if one combines that verse with Luke 1:28, "Hail, full of grace, the Lord is with you!" one can see that the first half of the beloved "Hail Mary" prayer is taken directly from Scripture.

[88] www.catholic.org

[89] "The Church's devotion to the Blessed Virgin is intrinsic to Christian worship." (Pope Paul VI, *Marialis cultus*, 56.) This devotion is not *laetria* (worship), but *hyperdulia* (the highest veneration or honor).

First, in imitation of God, who in choosing her to be the mother of our Savior honored her more highly than we ever could. Such an honor is not to be taken lightly. Nor is the command of Jesus from the cross to His beloved disciple, ***"Behold, your mother."*** [90] From the cross, Jesus entrusts the care of His mother to His beloved disciple, who represents the Lord's beloved Church. To honor Mary is to honor our mother which, of course, is to keep the fourth commandment, "Honor your father and your mother." [91]

Second, Catholics honor or venerate Mary in keeping with the long and consistent practice of the people of God. Mary was with the apostles on the day of Pentecost. [92] The Church of the early centuries approached Mary in prayer, asking her intercession. Artwork in the catacombs in Rome is evidence of the great respect paid to Mary in the early years of the Church. Early Christian writers such as St. Irenaeus, who lived in the second century, saw ***Mary as the "new Eve,"*** for just as Eve's disobedience to God brought death into the world, Mary's "Yes" to God would bring new and eternal life into the world. "The knot of Eve's disobedience was untied by Mary's obedience: what the virgin Eve bound through her disbelief, Mary loosened by her faith." [93]

From the very first days of the Church, Christians have honored the Blessed Mother, seeing in her ***a model of discipleship and a faithful woman of prayer*** who never stops interceding for her children. For she, too, was given a command from the cross: "Woman, behold, your son!" [94] From that moment on, the Scriptures tell us, the beloved disciple "took her to his own home," [95] a striking image for

---

[90] John 19:27.
[91] Exodus 20:12.
[92] Cf. Acts 1:14.
[93] St. Irenaeus, *Adversus Haereses* 3, 22, 4: PG 7/1, 959 A; quoted in CCC 494.
[94] John 19:26.
[95] John 19:27.

the affection and devotion Catholics have for the Blessed Mother to this very day.

The third point that struck Tony was that Catholics seek Mary's intercession under the prompting of the Holy Spirit, who teaches us how to pray.[96] The Holy Spirit directs us to pray to God not simply as individuals, but in communion with the Church, the Body of Christ. Even in our personal, silent prayer we do not pray alone. We pray in the name of Jesus, by the power of the Holy Spirit, and in the communion of the Church.[97] Is it any wonder that the Holy Spirit, who draws us together into that communion, would in the process draw us close to the Blessed Mother? Yes, we pray to her, for when we do, ***we pray with her and she with us.*** Just as we do not hesitate to ask our friends and fellow parishioners to pray for us in time of need, neither do we hesitate to ask the Blessed Mother for her intercession, her prayers.

Tony was not able to convince the campus proselytizers of his convictions, but he went to bed that night more assured of his beliefs and more convinced of the wisdom of the Catholic faith that had been passed on to him by his parents and grandparents, the faith he professes personally and proudly. Tony slept easily that night, but not before saying a prayer for those who waver in their faith and for those who are misguided in their zeal for the Lord, that they will one day come to appreciate and cherish the fullness of truth that is to be found in the Catholic faith. He asked the intercession of Mary, Mother of our Savior, Mother of God.

As we prepare to celebrate Christmas, may we be mindful of those who are away from the Church or at odds with her. Striving to be good stewards of the gift of faith, may we seek the intercession of Mary our Mother, praying, ***"Hail Mary ..."***

✠ **The Fourth Sunday of Advent (C)**
December 24, 2000

---

[96] Cf. CCC 2672.
[97] Cf. CCC 2664-2672.

Being Pro-Life
in a Rock-Solid Way

Showing respect for the dignity of the human person and speaking out for life in the political process are responsibilities of every steward. The annual observance of Respect Life Sunday is nothing less than a call to stewardship of human life.

Jesus gives Simon the brother of Andrew a new name: *Cephas* [98] in Aramaic. The same name is rendered *Petrus* in Greek and Latin, *Peter* in our language. *Cephas* means "rock": not a pebble or stone, but a massive rock like the Rock of Gibraltar, a rock that is going to be around for a good, long while.

Cephas: Rock. A fitting name for the apostle who would be the earthly head of the Church after our Lord's ascension into heaven. "You are Rock," Jesus would say to Simon Peter, "and upon this Rock I will build my Church, and the gates of hell will not prevail against it."[99]

The Church that the Lord Jesus establishes is a *Church that is built upon a rock-solid foundation.* The Church does not allow herself to be swayed by opinion polls or the latest ways of thinking. She stands firm in upholding the truth: the truth about Jesus, the truth about the sacraments, the truth about the dignity of the human person, which includes being...

... created in the image and likeness of God [100]
... endowed with an immortal soul [101]
*... given an innate dignity from conception
      until natural death.*[102]

---

[98] Note that *Cephas* is pronounced with a hard "c", like the "k" in *keep*.
[99] Cf. Matthew 16:18.
[100] Cf. CCC 355, quoting Genesis 1:27.
[101] Cf. CCC 363.

This is the truth. *And truth endures.* What is true today is true tomorrow, no matter how much a person might want it to be otherwise. This is the case in mathematics. Two plus two equals four. This is the truth today, as it was yesterday, and as it will be tomorrow. This is the case in science. Two atoms of hydrogen combine with one atom of oxygen to form water: H_2O. This is the truth now, as it always has been and always will be. And this is the case in natural law (morality). *The direct and voluntary killing of an innocent human being is always gravely immoral. This truth endures.* No manner of wishful thinking can make it otherwise. Nor can a decision of the Supreme Court.

This Wednesday tens of thousands of citizens will march on our behalf in Washington D.C. to make known their opposition, as well as our own, to the now thirty-year old *Roe v Wade* decision of the Supreme Court. That decision opened the floodgates for abortion-on-demand in our country. An estimated 40 million abortions have been performed since 1973, and the body count continues to rise. Forty million lives and counting! All of those innocent lives were destroyed under the protection of the law of the land. *There is no greater sorrow* than this, no greater tragedy than the fact that the flames of the silent holocaust rage on.

(I know this is a difficult subject for some of us. Perhaps some here today have experienced first-hand the sin of abortion. My words are not intended to cause further pain, but rather to speak the truth, however difficult it may be to hear. Yet I would be remiss if I did not remind all of us that *there is no sin that the Lord cannot or will not forgive.* With the Lord there is mercy and forgiveness. The Lord hates the sin, but loves the sinner. Turn to Him in the Sacrament of Penance and you will begin to find peace.)

On the occasion of the anniversary of the *Roe v Wade* decision, people of faith are praying that a change will occur:

---

[102] Cf. CCC 1700.

We pray that wise judges will be appointed and that they will stand up for the truth about the human person.

We pray that legislators and members of Congress will see through the rhetoric of choice, and that they will enact laws that affirm the dignity of the human person from conception until natural death.

We pray that more citizens will make their voices heard, and that they will not allow those in politics to remain lukewarm to the cause of the truth. It is not enough for someone holding or seeking public office to say, "I am personally opposed to abortion, but I will permit it as a matter of choice." That doesn't cut it. *Truth endures.* Truth is worth standing up for. Truth is worth fighting for.

On the issue of the dignity of the human person, we are called to good stewardship of the gift of human life. We must never back away from our responsibility as Catholic citizens; we must demand accountability from those in public office, holding their feet to the fire when necessary. We must make our voices known. We must not allow even decades-long party loyalty to keep us from standing up for the truth. Tolerating legalized abortion-on-demand is the single greatest blemish on the reputation of our nation. It violates and mocks our reputation for equal justice under the law. It is a malignancy. If left to grow it will suck the life, the very soul, from our beloved country.

Like St. Peter the Rock and like the Church, built on a *rock-solid* foundation, we are called to be *rock-solid* in our opposition to abortion. We are called to be *unambiguously pro-life.* [103]

Let us support the good work of our local Right to Life organizations. Let us stand up and be counted at the polls.

---

[103] This descriptive phrase was first used at the May 2000 funeral of John Cardinal O'Connor in praise of this champion of the Respect Life movement.

Let us make known in our community that there are *always* alternatives to abortion.

I call upon the young people of our parish to be leaders in getting this word out. Those who are in high school are on the front lines of the pro-life movement. You could be friends with a classmate who might one day make a mistake. That person might come to you for advice, even before seeking the counsel of a teacher or parent. When you are approached for advice, please communicate gently but firmly that abortion is *always* wrong and that there are *always* alternatives.

. If your friend needs help but doesn't know where to turn, please remember that we at St. Louis Parish are here to help. We care about babies and we care about expectant mothers. As a parish we will do *anything necessary* to help a young person in trouble to bring her baby to term. We will help with medical care, housing and, if appropriate, with adoption placement. Young people, please carry this message to the front lines: There are *always* alternatives to abortion.

In a few moments we will be nourished in Holy Communion by the Lord Jesus, Body and Blood, Soul and Divinity. May our sharing in the Holy Eucharist give us the strength we need to be *rock-solid* in our defense of the dignity of the human person. And by the witness and prayers of everyone in the pro-life movement *may our nation be renewed* in her dedication to truth and justice.

✠ **The Second Sunday in Ordinary Time (B)**
January 19, 2003

Fools for Christ

Though sometimes regarded as a fool because of his or her countercultural way of life, the steward strives to be conformed to the high standards of the Gospel. The virtue of courage is indispensable for the one who strives to follow the Lord.

I have a quote for you: **"God assumed from the beginning that the wise of the world would view Christians as fools – and He has not been disappointed."** I'll tell you who said that in just a few minutes.

From the very beginning of the Church, Christians have been regarded as fools. We believe that the Son of God was born of a virgin. We believe that Jesus rose from the dead and that He bodily ascended into heaven. We believe in miracles. We believe that those who obey God will rise from the dead to live in glory in heaven, and those who do not will burn in hell. We believe that marriage is for keeps, and that it's wrong to live together outside of marriage. We believe that contraception is sinful. We believe that life begins at conception and that no court in the land can make it otherwise.

And what does the world think about us for our beliefs? The answer is simple. **The world thinks us to be absolutely foolish.** Need proof?

Just turn on the television sometime. Count the number of characters who are presented as being attractive, poised, happy. Now, how many of them are presented as being people of faith? People who go to church? People who keep the commandments? It's exactly the opposite, isn't it? With but a few exceptions, there is an absence of faith in the lives of these people. Furthermore, it seems so common for television characters to flaunt their disregard of the commandments and laugh at those who keep them.

In our world the followers of Jesus Christ are not regarded as being popular. *We are not seen as being in the mainstream, and we are not viewed as wise.* Unless, of course, we dissent from our Church, explain away the key teachings of our faith, and live lives at odds with objective standards of morality. Then we become very popular, and quite savvy in the eyes of the world. Isn't it funny how it works that way? It's been working that way ever since the Romans threw the first Christians to the lions. And it will go on being that way until the Lord Jesus comes in glory.[104]

Here's that quote again: *"God assumed from the beginning that the wise of the world would view Christians as fools ... and He has not been disappointed."* These are the words of Supreme Court Justice Antonin Scalia, who spoke last week to a group of fellow Catholics at a Knights of Columbus dinner in Louisiana. He encouraged them (us) to *keep the faith in spite of ridicule* and in spite of the fact that the world is against us.

We will be called fools, Justice Scalia said. However, "intellect and reason need not be laid aside for religion. ... It is not irrational to accept the testimony of eyewitnesses who had nothing to gain"[105] (in reference to the eyewitnesses of the resurrection of Jesus). And it is certainly not irrational to follow the teaching of Jesus and His Church.

Justice Scalia concluded: "Have the *courage* to have your wisdom regarded as stupidity. Be fools for Christ. And have the *courage* to suffer the contempt of the civilized world."[106]

---

[104] Cf. John 16:33.

[105] Baton Rouge *Advocate*. "Faithful live for Christ: Supreme Court Justice urges Christian to live fearlessly" by Penny Brown Roberts. January 23, 2005, p. 1.A.

[106] Ibid., emphasis added.

These are words that the steward needs to hear. As St. Paul says, we must remember who we are, and to whom we belong.[107]   We must hold on to the faith that comes to us from the apostles, **no matter what the world says of our beliefs.** We must live according to the clear moral teachings of Jesus and the Church, no matter how much we might stand out from the crowd.

Why? Because our Lord is all together trustworthy.[108] We believe Him. And **we follow Him because His words are true, and His path is the way to heaven.**

That we might become more courageous, we are drawn this day to the banquet of the Lord. We participate in the Holy Sacrifice of the Mass and are nourished with the Body and Blood, Soul and Divinity of the Lord – all so that our faith might be strong enough to withstand the ridicule, the jeers, and the contempt of the world.

A faithful, devout Catholic college student was once asked "Why don't you party like everyone else? Why do you and your girlfriend remain chaste? Why don't you cheat to get good grades like the rest of us?" He responded, "Because I know who I am, and I know to whom I answer in this world and the next." A courageous young man. Also a happy, healthy, holy young man.

May our participation in the Eucharist this day help us to be confident in living lives worthy of our calling, in other words -- **to live life courageously.**

✠ **The Fourth Sunday in Ordinary Time (A)**
January 30, 2005

---

[107] Cf. 1Corinthians 6:19,20; 7:23; Galatians 2:20; 3:26-29.
[108] Cf. Proverbs 3:5.

The Holy Eucharist

Holy Thursday commemorates the institution of two great sacraments: the Holy Eucharist and Holy Orders. Through the priesthood, the Lord nourishes us for a life of stewardship with the precious gift of the Holy Eucharist, the Lord's very Body and Blood, Soul and Divinity.

We have come to the end of the 40 days of Lent, and now the Great Three Days begin, **The Paschal Triduum,** as these holy days are called.

Throughout Lent we have had occasion to consider the important things in life: things that last, things that are a matter of eternal life or eternal damnation. Through the power of the Sacrament of Penance we have been forgiven our sins, strengthened by God's grace, and sent forth as Jesus sent the woman caught in adultery, "to go and sin no more."[109]

Through the Sacrament of Penance and the penitential nature of the Lenten season **we have embraced the cross** of the Lord Jesus. **We have drawn near** to the font of the Lord's forgiveness, the wellspring of Divine Mercy. In admitting our sins and our weaknesses, **we have availed ourselves of the healing** that only the Great Physician can provide – the only doctor who can do our troubled souls any good at all.

Now we enter into the Solemn Commemoration of our Lord's Death and Resurrection. We enter into the depths of the mystery of God's plan for our redemption. By keeping these three days holy, and by engaging in the Liturgy of the Church, we are drawn even closer to the Lord. **We take our place at table** with Him at the Last Supper. **We watch one hour** with Him in the garden. **We walk with Him** on the

---

[109] Cf. John 8:11.

Via Dolorosa, the sorrowful way through the streets of Jerusalem. We take our place with Mary and John at the foot of the cross. *We die with the Lord* and experience the days of silence when "the Great King sleeps."[110] Then, and only then, do *we rise with the Lord,* who rises from the dead never to die again.

In this Liturgy at this threshold of the Paschal Triduum, *we remember* that on the night He was betrayed Jesus instituted *two sacraments,* through which He would keep for all ages His solemn promise "I am with you always, even until the end of the age."[111]

Jesus instituted the Holy Eucharist. Jesus partakes of the Passover meal, the meal by which He and His apostles had always remembered the saving power of God, the night when the children of Israel were saved by the blood of the lamb on their doorposts. That was the night when the children of Israel ate and drank with loins girt and sandals fastened, ready to depart the slavery to which they had been subjected for 400 years, ready to venture forth across the desert to find the Promised Land that God had in store for them.

When He presided over the meal in the presence of His apostles, Jesus faithfully and reverently fulfilled the Passover ritual as set forth by God so many generations ago. And then, in the middle of that time-tested ritual, *Jesus changed the words.* In blessing and breaking the unleavened bread, Jesus said, "Take and eat, this is My Body."[112] And in blessing and distributing the chalice of wine, Jesus said, "Take and drink, this is My blood."[113] At that defining moment, Jesus' last supper became the *First Eucharist.* Jesus' final Passover

---

[110] From *The Office of Readings* for Holy Saturday.
[111] Cf. Matthew 28:20.
[112] Cf. Matthew 26:26.
[113] Cf. Matthew 26:27,28.

meal became the **First Mass,** the first of countless others that would follow in every age and in every land.

Just as the apostles did that night, we on this night enter into a solemn communion with the Lord Jesus, a blood oath, as it were. By this new covenant His Body and Blood enter into our very persons so that in the manner of digestion, **His** Body and Blood becomes **our** flesh and blood. Jesus institutes the Eucharist not only so that bread and wine will change **but also that we will change,** so that we will become what we celebrate. Christ dwells within us that we might become:

- more **Christ-like** in our words and actions
- more **Christ-like** in our attitudes and thoughts
- more **Christ-like** in our willingness to be stewards for the sake of the Kingdom, even to embracing suffering and death as did our Master before us.

Jesus instituted the Holy Eucharist that sacred night, and so too did He institute the sacrament by which He would provide for the continuation of that same Eucharist. *Jesus instituted the Sacrament of Holy Orders* on that night before He died so that the Church would be nourished until the day of His return in glory. His apostles became the first priests, ordained to live their lives wholeheartedly for the sake of the Body of Christ. They were commissioned to be stewards of the Church, caring for, preserving, and sharing the gifts of Word and Sacrament.

Jesus entrusts the care of His Church, the preaching of the Gospel and the administration of the sacraments, *not to men who are perfect,* but to men like Peter who would deny Him, and Thomas, who would doubt His resurrection, and to James and John who would not be able to watch even one hour with Him in the garden. Jesus would entrust His Church to men who themselves would need to rely every day upon the mercies of the Lord, the prayers of the community of believers, and the intercession of all the saints of heaven.

The Church continues to be built up by the leadership of the bishops as the successors of the apostles, and by the ministry of priests and deacons, who serve as the co-workers of the bishops. *Only by the daily action of the Holy Spirit can this holy endeavor be sustained;* only in a manner wholly born from God's grace can our Church survive, let alone thrive.

Let us praise our God tonight for the good work He accomplishes through His less-than-perfect instruments, His humble stewards, the priests of the Church. Let us praise God for bestowing upon the priests who serve us the grace they need to persevere in their calling.

Let us ask the Lord to visit with mercy those priests who have fallen.

Let us ask the Lord to strengthen and heal those priests who are discouraged or who suffer any form of illness.

And let us call upon the Lord to raise up from our own parish young men of strong faith and steadfast conviction who will not turn away when they hear the words "Come, follow Me."[114]

May our young men be attentive to the sound of the voice of Jesus who calls not the perfect, and not even the brightest and the best. Rather, *Jesus calls whom He chooses* for a life of service, a life of adventure (for there is never a dull moment), and life truly worth living, a life I would not trade for any earthly treasure.

Please God may we keep these three days well. May we look back over these forty days of Lent and praise God for the blessings we have received. May we humbly partake of

---

[114] Cf. Matthew 4:19.

the Holy Eucharist this holy night, receiving the great gift of the Lord's Body and Blood, Soul and Divinity. May we be ever grateful that the Lord keeps in this way His solemn promise, *"Lo I am with you always, even to the end of the age."* [115]

✠ **Holy Thursday 2003**
April 17, 2003

Cast Your Nets Starboard

The steward spends a lifetime learning the importance of relying always upon the guidance and direction of the Lord. The risen Lord Jesus teaches His apostles, and He teaches us, that He is always near, especially in time of need.

The apostles learn at least three things in the appearance of the Risen Lord Jesus on the shore of the Sea of Galilee.

First, they learn that Jesus is present when their nets are empty. *Jesus is present in their need.*

Let's be clear about something. The apostles were hard workers. They had fished all night long, using all their experience and skill to bring in the catch, but they had nothing to show for their work. Their nets were empty.

Sometimes we find ourselves in similar situations. We work hard, we labor diligently, but we still come up empty. The new job with all the prestige and the great salary doesn't bring fulfillment. The son or daughter who is deeply loved doesn't show gratitude and is, in fact, resentful and bitter. The marriage seemingly made in heaven now languishes in

---

[115] Cf. Matthew 28:20.

anger over the sin of infidelity. Despite out best intentions and our hard work, our nets can be empty, our hearts disappointed and sad.

Every life has its sorrows, its emptiness. When we face such times in our lives, we can do no better than to recall the empty nets of the apostles, and to remember that in their time of need Jesus was there. And so it is today. In our darkest hours, *Jesus is there.* St. Paul reminds us that nothing can separate us from the love of Christ: "Neither death, nor life, nor angels, nor principalities, nor things present, nor things to come, ... will be able to separate us from the love of God in Christ Jesus our Lord."[116]

What does the resurrection mean? It means that *Jesus is there, especially when the nets are empty.* That is the first thing that the apostles learn about the resurrection.

The *second* thing they learn is that *Jesus is there to teach,* to instruct, to offer direction. Jesus is not there to offer empty sympathy. He is there to make a difference.

"Cast your nets starboard and you will catch something,"[117] they hear a stranger say. Imagine their reaction! Seven professional fishermen, tired from fishing all night long, and they hear a stranger offering advice. (Remember, they had not yet recognized that it was Jesus.) Can you imagine their response? Yet with great humility, they lower their nets. "Obviously, we don't have all the answers," they say. "Perhaps we can benefit from the stranger's counsel."

What a difference it made that they had listened and taken direction from the Risen Lord. The Church to this very day continues to celebrate that miraculous catch! And the Church continues to be profoundly aware that the

---

[116] Romans 8:38,39.
[117] Cf. John 21:6.

resurrection means that *Jesus is alive,* and that He continues to teach, to instruct, to guide. His words give us the direction we need in life. *His words make the difference* between despair and hope, between emptiness and abundance.

We hear His words in the Scriptures and in the teachings of the Church. His word is altogether reliable and true. And yet at times His word sounds out of place to us, just as did the unsolicited advice of the stranger on the seashore. "What do you mean, cast your nets starboard?" the apostles thought. And so today the teaching of the Church can strike us as unsolicited advice, especially on topics such as care for the poor, cohabitation, contraception, capital punishment, and so on. Jesus' words are not always well-taken. And yet what a difference it makes when we put His words into practice, when we cast our nets starboard and trust in His guidance, His direction, His instruction.

The resurrection means that *He is with us* and that *He gives us the words that make a difference.* The apostles learn those two lessons on the shore of the Sea of Galilee. They also learn a *third* lesson: *The Risen Lord Jesus makes Himself known in the Breaking of the Bread.*

The image of the Risen Lord offering His apostles an early morning meal on the shore of the sea is a beautiful image of the Eucharist. When we are tired and weary, Jesus feeds us with His Body and Blood. Jesus gives us not only His instruction, *He gives us His presence* in a real and substantial way through the Holy Eucharist.

What does the resurrection mean? It means that Jesus keeps His sacred promise: "I am with you always, even to the end of the age."[118] He keeps that promise precisely by giving us the gift of the Eucharist, His Body and Blood, Soul and Divinity, the Bread of Life and the Cup of Eternal Salvation. *Through the Eucharist we receive the strength we need*

---

[118] Cf. Matthew 28:20.

to persevere in our faith and to accomplish all that the Lord asks us to do in life.

Jesus cares about us, just as He cared about the outcome of His apostles' fishing expedition. He is there for us in time of need. He gives us words of wisdom and He feeds us with the only food that truly satisfies the hungry heart. The faithful steward learns to trust in the enduring presence of the Lord.

That is the good news of the resurrection, for the apostles and for each and every one of us. May we never be too proud to heed the Lord's timeless counsel: *"Cast your nets starboard."*

✠ **The Third Sunday of Easter 2001 (C)**
April 29. 2001

Priestly Celibacy

Priestly celibacy is a gift to the one who is called to Holy Orders and is a gift to the Church. A mark of good stewardship is respect, support and encouragement of the gift of celibacy for the sake of the Kingdom.

The Fourth Sunday of Easter is called "Good Shepherd Sunday." The Scriptures speak of Jesus in the familiar and comforting image of the Good Shepherd[119] who knows His sheep and calls them each by name. He leads them through the valley of the shadow of death to verdant pastures and restful waters. *The Good Shepherd comes so that the*

---

[119] Psalm 23; John 10:1-18.

sheep might have life and have it in abundance. He is single-hearted in His service to the flock.

Our Holy Father designates Good Shepherd Sunday as the World Day of Prayer for Vocations. We pray especially for those who are shepherds in our Church today, our bishops and priests. We pray for men who are in the seminary (including two of our own parishioners) and for young men who are discerning the call.

On this Good Shepherd Sunday I wish to speak about a particular aspect of priestly life that is a great blessing for our Church and for our world, and yet which is being called into question more and more. *I speak of the gift of priestly celibacy.*

I use the term *gift* deliberately. *The call to celibacy is a gift of God given to the priest* so that he might live a life of total dedication to priestly service. In turn, *celibacy is a gift to the Church and the world,* for through it the priest is able to imitate Christ Jesus, the Good Shepherd, in service that is single-hearted.

The gift of celibacy is much misunderstood, even by otherwise loyal Catholics. A number of very solid articles have been published recently by both Catholic and non-Catholic writers, dispelling the notion that celibacy is the cause of the problems in the headlines these days.[120] However, we still hear an ongoing mantra from many Catholics: "It is only a matter of time before priestly celibacy will be optional if not non-existent."

"After all, celibacy is a medieval relic. It has only been Church law for the last 900 years, there are married priests in the Eastern rites, and furthermore, the only reason a priest doesn't marry is that he wouldn't have time for both his

---

[120] This homily was preached at the height of the revelation of clergy scandals in 2002.

family and his parish. A better system of time management could solve that problem," so they say.

Oh really? Is *that* all priestly celibacy is? An archaic medievalism that can be disposed of without serious consequence to our Church? I sure hope not. I hope that the solemn promise I made when I was ordained fourteen years ago and the life that I continue to lead is more than an affectation of a bygone era.

Let's take a good look at priestly celibacy:

Priestly celibacy goes back not 900 years, but to our Lord Himself, who never married. And although some of the apostles may have been married (remember that Simon Peter's mother-in-law is mentioned in the Gospels), it is indisputable that Jesus called them to a single-hearted service.

Jesus says, "There is no one who has left house or brothers or sisters or mother or father or children or lands, for my sake and for the gospel, who will not receive a hundredfold now in this time, houses and brothers and sisters and mothers and children and lands, with persecutions, and in the age to come eternal life."[121]

St. Paul praises "the men of faith who live a celibate life and who ... consecrate themselves with undivided heart to the Lord and to 'the affairs of the Lord.' "[122]

And while it is true that the Church has, and in fact does ordain as priests married men, she has never permitted a priest to marry and continue in the priestly service. There has always been and always will be a consciousness in the Church of the importance of priestly celibacy.

Why is this the case?

---

[121] Mark 10:29, 30.
[122] 1Corinthians 7:32, quoted in CCC 1579. This does not mean that priests have always been chosen from the ranks of celibate men, but to assert that priestly celibacy is only 900 years old is historically inaccurate.

First, through celibacy priests are configured to Jesus Christ in a profound way, allowing them to be single-hearted in service of the Lord and His Church. It is deeper than a "time management" issue, i.e. a priest not having time or energy for both family and parish. Through living the celibate life, a priest is able to be consecrated to the Lord, and that consecration, that single-heartedness, allows the priest to be at the service of not just one family, but every family.

Second, through their commitment to celibacy, priests offer a living witness to the power of faith. Priests point to that which is unseen but lasting, that which is invisible but eternal. A priest who embraces celibacy and lives it faithfully says to the Church and the world: "Even though celibacy may seem to be absurd in the eyes of the world, I put my trust in the Lord who will be my joy and my peace for all eternity."

If there are fewer men entering seminaries these days, I don't think that it is because marriage and family have somehow become more appealing than ever before. I think numbers are down because of a crisis of faith in the family. *The greatest seedbed for vocations to the priesthood has always been the family.*

I am grateful that a few years ago, when a grade school boy expressed the desire to be a priest, a certain family affirmed that decision and supported him through twelve years of discernment. They did not push, but they quietly told that young man that if the call were truly from God, then *the Lord would provide happiness in this life and happiness beyond measure in the life to come.* That family was my family, and I will be ever grateful.

Finally, the Church will always be conscious of the importance of priestly celibacy because of our lived experience of *the power of a priest's life to be generative and paternal* in its own way. We call our priests "Father" for a reason. Celibacy enables priests to be spiritual fathers of so many people in ways that are known only to the Lord. I have experienced and continue to experience great contentment and peace knowing that through Holy Orders I am ***spiritually a life-giver.*** God has given me this great gift, a gift that you affirm every time that you address me as "Father." For that I am tremendously grateful.

I do not regret answering the call to become a priest. There are difficult moments, yes, but probably not more than in other walks of life. Celibacy sometimes brings with it the cross of loneliness, but more often it brings me the satisfaction of knowing that every day I am doing something of great importance for building up the Kingdom of God.

I place my trust in a God who is absolutely reliable, and I trust that God will give me and my brother priests the grace we need to live out the priestly vocation in a chaste and celibate way. I rely upon your prayers, believe me! I know that through God's grace my vocation as a celibate priest will never stop being the life-giving and exceptionally fulfilling life that it is for me today.

✠ **The Fourth Sunday of Easter (A)**
April 21, 2002

A Vocations Shortage?

There is no vocation shortage. There is a shortage in those who respond to God's call. God blesses many families with the gift of children, and every parent with the responsibility of nurturing the faith and vocation of each child. Parents are good stewards of these blessings when they pray for and support vocations to the priesthood and religious life, a generous response to God.

A pastor once took to the pulpit and told his parishioners: "We have a problem. The roof is leaking. It has been repaired time and time again. This time it needs to be replaced. The cost will be $200,000." There was an audible gasp in the congregation. Then the pastor said, "I have some good news and some bad news. The good news: we have the money. The bad news: it's still in your pockets."

My friends, our roof is not leaking and even though there is a second collection today for seminary education, I'm not here to talk about money. But I do want you to know that we have a problem. *A happy problem.* The number of Catholics in our area and throughout the country is increasing. Furthermore, Catholics, especially young Catholics, are taking their faith quite seriously. There is an increase in demand for the sacraments of the Church, especially the Sacrament of Penance. There is an increasing demand for good teaching and pastoral presence in our parishes and in our schools.

The bottom line is that if our Church is going to thrive, *we need more priests and religious to serve the Church.* Now I have some good news and some bad news. The good news is that contrary to what you might have heard, there is *not* a vocation shortage. If fact, *there is a vocation surplus.* God is not being stingy with vocations. The good news is that we have a surplus of vocations to serve the Church. The bad news is that *they are still in your homes.*

Now that's not *really* bad news, is it? In your homes, among your children and grandchildren, your brothers and sisters are young people for whom God has some very special plans. *Some in your family are being called* to an extraordinary way of loving and serving God as religious — and they have the potential to change the world. Where would we be without St. Vincent Hospital, St. Augustine's Home for the Aged and our Catholic schools, all of which were and are built up by the dedication, care and love of our religious. Where would we be without the tens of thousands of religious who anonymously and without fanfare perform a ministry of prayer and humble service. Those men and women of faith who live very simple, holy lives have changed and are changing the world. Some in your family are being called to that way of life and can find great happiness in it. That is good news!

Some of your sons, grandsons and brothers are being called to serve at the altar, to stand in the person of Christ, to effect the miraculous change of bread and wine into our Lord's Body and Blood. Through their priestly ministry they will change hearts, drawing others closer to the Lord. That is good news!

A couple of years ago a grandmother wrote a letter to each of her children and grandchildren expressing beautifully her love for our Catholic faith and her prayer that at least one person in her family would serve the Church as a priest or religious. The wisdom of her years tells her that vocations do not come out of thin air. *Vocations are nurtured in an atmosphere of good stewardship in the home, in the family.* For in the family a very important lesson is learned over and over again: God provides. God takes care of us. God gives us strength to carry our crosses. And in the Lord do we find our true happiness.

That very wise and faith-filled grandmother gives me cause to be optimistic about the future of our Church, optimistic that we will have the priests and religious we need. My hopes are further edified when I see the quality of young men and women who are inquiring about vocations and enrolling in seminaries and religious orders.

Last evening I had the privilege of being at St. Barnabas on the Southside for a presentation given by "Bikers for Jesus." Twelve new graduates from the college seminary in St. Paul, Minnesota, chose to offer thanks for their college experience by bicycling from St. Paul to Evansville, Indiana, stopping each day at a different parish, telling their listeners of their love for Jesus and inviting others to consider carefully the call to the priesthood or religious life. What an impressive task and a powerful witness! And these men are still four years away from ordination! They are bright, articulate, talented young men, just like many of your sons, grandsons, and brothers.

God is not being stingy with vocations, but sometimes the call is not heard or is lost through indifference or rejection. And what a shame. *I thank God for my calling.* I thank God for all those who prayed for me along the way and who still pray for me now. I thank God that my family was close to the Church and that the seeds of my vocation were given encouragement to grow and develop. I thank God for the happiness and satisfaction I find as a priest. *Priesthood is my calling* and I cannot imagine myself finding that same level of happiness anywhere else. The Lord provides. And *He provides in abundance!*

Please join me today in supporting seminary education through the second collection and in hope-filled prayers for vocations to the priesthood and religious life. We will pray for vocations publicly at our Corpus Christi procession and will continue to do so at our monthly Holy Hour.

I invite you to join me right after Communion in praying in the quiet of your heart, praying by name for specific individuals who would make good priests or religious. The time after Communion is fitting for after I receive and distribute the Body and Blood of our Lord in Holy Communion, I pray that others will respond to the call to serve at the altar – so that the sacrifice of the Mass might continue to be offered.

The good news is that we have the vocations we need as a Church. *The further good news* is that they are in your families.

✠ **Feast of Corpus Christi 1999 (A)**
June 6, 1999

Keep Your Eyes Fixed on Jesus

College students preparing to return for the fall semester were challenged in this homily to live their faith on campus in a vibrant and authentic manner. They were challenged to keep their eyes fixed on Jesus and to be good and faithful stewards by nurturing the gift of faith and sharing it generously with others.

S ad to say, *we sometimes take our faith for granted.* We attend church, for an hour on Sunday and yet at times that hour does not truly consecrate the week to God. We might leave church unaffected by our Holy Communion with the Lord Jesus, resuming our daily activities without giving much thought to how being a person of faith is supposed to make a difference.

Sadly, we sometimes take our faith for granted. We have so many other influences in our lives, telling us what is right, what is good, what is important, drowning out the truth of the Gospel. It's hard for one hour in Church each week to make much of a difference. Before long, even that one hour per week begins to slip to every other week, or once a month, or just Christmas and Easter. *Faith begins to atrophy,* and becomes more a nostalgic or cultural event, rather than a real conviction about powerful things unseen.

The Church teaches that participation in Sunday Mass[123] is a serious obligation for all Catholics who are able to attend. We need to consecrate the Lord's Day by drawing near to the Eucharistic Lord Jesus. We need this weekly connection to the Lord Jesus and to His Body, the Church. Even if we "don't get anything out of it", giving one hour per week to the God who gives us life seems to be a pretty good bargain.

---

[123] The Sunday Mass obligation may also be met by attending the Saturday evening Mass of anticipation.

Attending Sunday Mass is the obligation, the "minimum weekly requirement" as it were. But *the Church urges us to do more than the minimum.* Daily morning and evening prayer is important in keeping our faith active and dynamic. Daily Mass is a great consolation along with regular confession and devotional prayer such as the rosary. Reading and discussing the Scriptures and praying with friends in a small group can be a wonderful way of keeping one's faith in Jesus Christ strong and vibrant.

The Letter to the Hebrews presents a good verse about keeping our faith strong: "Let us run with perseverance the race that is set before us, *looking to Jesus* the pioneer and perfecter of our faith"[124]

"Keep your eyes fixed on Jesus" the scriptures say. Keep Him as your goal and your guide and everything will be fine. We might remember the image of St. Peter, who was able to walk upon the water all the while keeping his eyes fixed upon Jesus. But when distracted, he began to sink, only to be pulled into the boat by the loving arms of the Lord.[125]

Keep your eyes fixed on Jesus day in and day out. Remain vigilant in prayer and attentive and alert to the Word of God. Do not take the faith for granted, but cherish it and exercise it every day through prayer, study, and by being true to the commandments. When faith is taken for granted, it atrophies. When exercised, faith becomes strong.

This is a message for all of us, to be sure, but it is a message that I want to give especially to those leaving for college this week. *Keep your eyes fixed on Jesus* and you will honor the Lord and you will grow strong in body, mind and spirit.

---

[124] Hebrews 12:1-2, emphasis added.
[125] Cf. Matthew 14:29-31.

College is a time when many abandon their faith. Religion is looked down upon in certain circles. New friends might not give one much encouragement to go to church or take the teachings of the Church seriously.

But the college years provide a unique and wonderful opportunity for a student to develop every facet of his or her person, including (and especially) the spiritual side. *Three points in particular:*

Number one:. Make friends with *those who are supportive of faith in general and the Catholic faith specifically.* Meet the friends you can find in the library, friends with names like Augustine, Aquinas, More, Newman and Chesterton. Make friends as well with the brilliant pope from Poland who brought down the Iron Curtain and who, despite halting voice and trembling hand enjoys a deep connection with young people.[126] His writings offer a powerful antidote to the despair and nihilism of our modern era. Do not let your faith atrophy, but exercise your faith through diligent study.

Number two: *Live in a way that respects your human dignity* and the dignity of everyone you meet. College means more freedom, to be sure, but *freedom is not a license* to do whatever you want, it is the ability to do what is right. "Do not be conformed to this world but be transformed by the renewal of your mind, that you may prove what is the will of God, what is good and acceptable and perfect."[127]

Number three: You will learn much in the classroom and in the laboratory. But you will learn even more through the practices of daily prayer, and if possible, daily Mass. *Turn to the Lord,* keep your eyes fixed on Jesus and you will learn the great plans He has in store for you. *Be good and faithful*

---

[126] See footnote 74.
[127] Romans 12:2.

stewards of God's manifold gifts. Be open to His will and your hearts will never be disappointed.

May our participation in the Eucharist this day help us to keep our eyes fixed upon Jesus, the leader and perfecter of our faith, a faith that we must never take for granted.

✠ **The Twentieth Sunday in Ordinary Time (C)**
   August 19, 2001

Priest, Prophet, and King

The Church, established upon the rock of St. Peter, is the means by which the Lord Jesus teaches, guides, and sanctifies His flock. The good steward is always grateful for the enduring vitality of the Church, giving thanks for God's gift of self in Jesus.

When Jesus came among us as God-made-man, he exercised the three offices of teaching, governing and sanctifying[128] the Church. We speak of Jesus first as *prophet or teacher,* second as *King or shepherd* of the flock, and third as *priest, the man of sacrifice.*

As teacher, His words of wisdom, compassion, consolation and challenge held the crowds spellbound, for he spoke with an authority unfamiliar to his listeners.[129]

Jesus **the Good Shepherd** restored the flock to wholeness. Not only did he bestow physical healing upon the

---

[128] Cf. CCC 873.
[129] Cf. Matthew 7:28,29; Mark 1:22; Luke 4:6.

blind, lame and mute, but He also healed individual souls and communities by forgiving sins and reconciling enemies.

Jesus is also *the great High Priest* who offered Himself as the perfect sacrifice. He humbled Himself of His divinity so as to share in our humanity. He gave of Himself for the sake of others, even to the point of giving His life on the cross,[130] all for the remission of our sins.

Jesus' earthly ministry of teaching, shepherding, and offering the great sacrifice is a ministry that He wanted to see continue after His ascension into heaven. And so Jesus established the Church, built with the twelve apostles as pillars, resting upon the immovable foundation of the rock of St. Peter. Jesus breathed the Spirit on the Apostles, and by the power of the Holy Spirit the mission of Christ is continued in the Church through the apostolic office.[131]

In the early days after Jesus' ascension, *we see two things happening in the Church.* First, the apostles exercised this same three-fold ministry, as they *taught* with authority, *shepherded* the Church in unity, and *sanctified* the early believers in the Holy Sacrifice of the Mass. Second, they ensured that Christ's ministry would continue by appointing successors through the laying-on of hands.

St. Peter and his successors occupy a unique role in the Church, one of primacy among the other disciples. Furthermore, Peter is singled out by Jesus as "the rock," the sure foundation upon which Jesus would build His Church, so unshakeable that even the gates of hell would not prevail against it.[132]

St. Peter the Rock served as the first bishop of Rome and was eventually martyred there. From the earliest days of the

---

130 Cf. Philippians 2:6-8
131 Cf. CCC 852.
132 Cf. Matthew 16:18,19.

Church his successors have been seen as ones who would lead for the sake of unity, settle disputes, teach with authority, even lay down their lives for the sake of the Church.

As good stewards, counting our many blessings from God, we have cause to be grateful for the office of the successor of St. Peter for several reasons:

We can be grateful that our Church has a central teaching authority, one that can hand on to us in an authentic manner the faith that comes from the apostles. Our world needs the clear and compelling moral vision of the successor to St. Peter, especially in its struggles with materialism, hedonism and nihilism.

We can be grateful that our Church is universal in scope, held together in unity by the pastoral zeal of Peter's successor. The very name *catholic* means universal – indicating that the Catholic Church is not just one Church of many, but the one Church established for all people and for all time by Christ Himself.

We can be grateful that our Church continues the legacy of the Lord's sacrifice. Pope John Paul II begins each day with intense prayer before the Blessed Sacrament followed by the celebration of the Holy Sacrifice of the Mass.[133] This sacramental connection with the Lord Jesus gives our Pope the grace he needs to inspire us to live our lives as stewards with dedication, with commitment, and with the willingness to do whatever it takes to live out our faith, even if that means laying down our lives for the sake of the Gospel.

Finally, we can be grateful that our Church will endure until the end of the age. Tyrants have tried to destroy the Church but have failed. Napoleon, Hitler, Stalin, and Mao have all inflicted great harm upon the Church, but

---

[133] See footnote 74.

they were unsuccessful in destroying her. Should we be surprised that the Evil One would continue to try to destroy the Church, not only from without, but from within? And yet we are promised by the Lord that the Church will be ever resilient, ever new, ever strong enough to withstand even the powers of hell.[134]

As we hold this promise of Jesus close to our hearts, *may we pray for the grace to remain loyal to the teachings of the Church* and faithful to her precepts. For it is in the Church that we do have a rock — a sure and stable foundation upon which to live our lives, build our future, and look to the hope of eternal life.

✠ **The Twenty-first Sunday in Ordinary Time (A)**
August 25, 2002

I Am the Bread of Life

"To whom shall we go, Lord, for you alone have the words of everlasting life?" The steward draws great strength from the Holy Eucharist, for there is the steward most closely united with the Lord, the Bread of Life, who gives Himself to us most fully in this sacred gift of His Body and Blood.

Today's Gospel[135] is the conclusion to the beautiful and profound part of the Bible that is *John, Chapter Six*. In this chapter Jesus refers to Himself as the Bread of Life: "I am the bread of life. The bread which I shall give for the life

---

[134] Ibid.
[135] John 6:60-69.

of the world is my flesh. Unless you eat the flesh of the Son of man and drink his blood, you have no life in you."[136] Strong words. Passionate words. Truthful words. *Jesus is teaching about Himself and the sacrificial death He is to endure. He is teaching about the Holy Eucharist,* the Sacrament by which the Sacrifice of the Cross is made present on the altars of the Church until the day He returns in glory.

What is the reaction of the disciples of Jesus to His clear and bold words? *How do they respond to His teaching?* The conclusion to John, Chapter Six tells us that they were shocked and offended. They murmured against Him. "Many of His disciples drew back and no longer went about with him."[137] His teaching was too much for them, and they left Him.

I find it very interesting to notice Jesus' reaction when He sees His closest followers taking their leave. *He does not change His message* in order to win them back. *He does not soften His teaching* so as to be more popular with the crowds. *He stands firm* in His teaching on the Bread of Life in spite of the consequences. He speaks the truth, unwavering and steadfast.

Contrast this with what would happen today if a person running for public office were to say some things that would cause his supporters to start murmuring and complaining. Imagine what would happen if the politician were to see his key supporters starting to break ranks because of something he said. Within moments the "damage control" would begin, with the *spinmeisters* claiming, "What our candidate *meant* to say ..." or "What our candidate *really* said ..."

You've seen that happen, haven't you? When someone seeking office loses popularity you can usually count on that

---

[136] John 6:35, 48, 51, 53.
[136] John 6:35, 48, 51, 53.
[137] John 6:66.

person to adapt his views and change his ideas so as to garner the widest possible support.

But is this what Jesus does? Not at all. *He makes clear His teaching and then sticks to His guns.*

He knows that *His words are controversial.* He knows that His listeners have great difficulty accepting that His Flesh and Blood are real food and real drink – the Bread of Life and the Cup of Eternal Salvation that is the Sacrament of the Holy Eucharist. He knows that *His words are scandalous,* for they point to what St. Paul would call "the scandal of the cross."[138] He knows that many will not be able to accept Him or His words. They will reject Him. Still, He does not relent. He does not cease speaking the truth.

He does, however, look at His closest disciples, His twelve apostles. And He asks them ever so gently, "Are you going to leave me, too?"[139]

Without the slightest hesitation St. Peter speaks for himself and for the apostles, and for the whole Church. In fact, *St. Peter speaks for you and me* when he answers, "Lord, to whom shall we go? You have the words of eternal life."[140]

It is the Lord Jesus who has the words of everlasting life.

It is the Lord Jesus who establishes the Church on the rock of St. Peter to preserve His holy words and to perpetuate His life and ministry through the administration of the Sacraments.

It is the Lord Jesus who gives to the Church the sacrament of Holy Orders so that priests might be ordained

---

138 Cf. Galatians 5:11.
139 Cf. John 6:67.
140 John 6:68.

to stand in His place at the altar and to offer in His person the Holy and Perfect Sacrifice of the Mass.

It is the Lord Jesus who gives us the Holy Eucharist as the specific means by which He would keep His solemn promise "Lo, I am with you always, to the close of the age."[141]

What happens then if we find His teachings difficult, and we are tempted to leave His Church, perhaps for a church with softer pews or softer moral teachings?

What happens if we are tempted to leave His Catholic Church for a church with more eloquent preachers, or a church with teachings that are easier on the ear?

What happens if we are tempted leave the Church that the Lord Jesus establishes perhaps for no church at all, but rather for the "sake of staying at home on Sunday" and "praying as I choose, just between God and me"?

What happens if we are tempted to shake the dust off our feet because of this scandal or that misdeed?

If one of those temptations occurs (God forbid), please remember how St. Peter answered our Lord at the very moment when so many of his cohorts were leaving. St. Peter said, and so should we, ***"Lord, to whom shall we go? You have the words of eternal life."*** [142]

There is nothing wrong with searching. It is good to search. It is good to be dedicated to seeking the truth.

Those who seek the truth will find the Truth, Jesus: The Way, the Truth, and the Life.[143]

Those who find Jesus find His sacred bride, the Catholic Church.

---

[141] Matthew 28:20.
[142] John 6:68.
[143] Cf. John 14:6.

Those who find the Catholic Church find the Holy Eucharist.

Those who find the Holy Eucharist find the Lord Jesus, ever faithful, His heart always open, abounding in mercy and love.

As we conclude our reading of John, Chapter Six, may we truly *be grateful for our faith in Jesus Christ, the Bread of Life and for the gift of the Holy Eucharist.* May we practice our Catholic faith – and practice it well—the faith that comes to us from the apostles.

✠ **The Twenty-first Sunday in Ordinary Time (B)**
August 24, 2003

Unambiguously Pro-Life

As the courageous martyrs of China were canonized, Catholics in the United States faced a setback in their efforts to keep the abortion pill (RU-486) off the market. The steward is not daunted by the culture of death, but remains unambiguously pro-life. Why? Because life is God's most precious gift to us and we have a sacred responsibility to care for it.

Some things are *more important than life or limb.*

The 120 martyrs of China canonized today bear witness to that. They gave their lives for the sake of the Kingdom of God in a period between 1648 and 1930. To this very day, Chinese Catholics are persecuted by the Communist authorities, suffering grave violations of their human rights, including imprisonment, beatings, and yes, even death itself.[144]

As attested to by the thin red line of martyr's blood throughout the history of the Church, some things are more important than life or limb.

This is the challenge Jesus puts before every steward in today's Gospel. Jesus challenges us to keep our priorities always in proper order, to **seek first the Kingdom of God,** [145] to keep our eyes fixed always on the good things of heaven.

Two great commandments direct us to do just that:

The first and greatest commandment is "You shall love the Lord your God with all your heart, and with all your soul, and with all your mind."[146]   "Love God above all else, serve Him and praise Him with every fiber of your being," Jesus would say to us today, "and you will find true blessedness in this life and eternal happiness in the life to come."

Some say that this is the greatest commandment because if we keep it well by making the love of God our top priority in life, then the other commandments are superfluous. As St. Paul says, "Love is the fulfilling of the Law."[147] (And as St. Augustine says, you should "love God and do what you will," for if we truly love God, then we will do the good.)

Jesus teaches us that the **second greatest commandment** is "You shall love your neighbor as yourself."[148] It is simply the other side of the coin of the

---

[144] See www.cardinalkungfoundation.org for more on the Catholic Church in China.

[145] Cf. Matthew 6:33.

[146] Matthew 22:37.

[147] Romans 13:10.

[148] Matthew 22:39.

greatest commandment. For if we love God, we will love, honor, and respect God's creation.

We must show the greatest respect for the entire created order, and we must be good stewards of the land, the water, the air, and all living creatures. Loving God the Creator means *honoring God's creation.* [149]

Of course, honoring God's creation entails honoring and loving the human person: the apex of God's creative powers, created in God's image and likeness.

Respect for human life fulfills the great challenge of the commandment, "Love your neighbor as yourself." To respect life is:

To protect and defend the life of the unborn child from the moment of conception, the moment when that child's unique genetic code is established, the moment when that child receives from God an immortal soul;

To extend pastoral care and God's mercy and forgiveness to those who have participated in the sin of abortion, assuring them that there is no sin so grievous that the Lord cannot or will not forgive;

To cherish the life of a person with a disability, recognizing that within each person one can discern the genius and love of the Creator;

To provide palliative and spiritual care to the person who is dying, patiently honoring that person's dignity through the hour of death, whenever it might come;[150]

To defend not only innocent human life, but also that of the guilty. Pope John Paul II reminds us that when non-lethal means are available to protect society from a violent criminal, the life of that criminal should be spared as a

---

149 Cf. CCC 2415-2418.
150 Cf. CCC 2299.

prophetic witness to the God-given dignity of every human person. If the life of the guilty person is protected by law, then how much more should the life of the innocent person in the womb be held as inviolable?[151]

Our Savior commands us to respect human life from the moment of conception until natural death. This is why our Church will never stop reminding us of our sacred duty to be, in every possible way, *unambiguously pro-life.*[152]

This is why our Church increasingly exercises her prophetic role in regard to life issues, speaking out against the law in Oregon that permits murder, albeit done under the softer name of *physician-assisted suicide.*

This is why our Church will not give up the fight against the alarming practice of *infanticide* (the murder of an infant), albeit done under the softer name of "partial-birth abortion." That the highest court in the land would strike down a prohibition against this most heinous and cruel practice should cause every citizen to take notice and to use his or her political clout to do something about it.

This is why our Church is deeply saddened at the action of the Food and Drug Administration this past Thursday in authorizing the sale of the *RU-486 pill.* Is it not a betrayal of the truth for the same man[153] who promised eight years ago to make abortion "safe, legal and rare" to applaud the legalization of a chemical that will only serve to make abortion more common than it already is? This chemical will grievously harm the physical, psychological and spiritual health of women. This chemical deserves not the honor of being called a medicine, but rather warrants the label *poison,* for it is poisonous to the life of the unborn, the health of the woman who uses it, and indeed the well-being of the society

---

[151] *Evangelium vitae,* no 56; also cf. CCC 2266, 2267, Second Edition.
[152] See footnote 103.
[153] President William Clinton.

we hold dear. That our president would sanction this terrible action should cause every citizen to take notice and to use his or her political clout to do something about it.

As Catholics we are called not to keep to ourselves, and not to be content with our "private morality." Rather we are called to be faithful to the command of Jesus: "Go therefore and make disciples of all nations ... **teaching** them to observe all that I have commanded you."[154]

We are called to evangelize –to spread the teachings of Jesus, especially that which Jesus taught as the **two greatest commandments**: "Love God with all your heart, mind, and soul, and love your neighbor as yourself."

We are called to evangelize individuals and we are called to **evangelize our culture,** bringing the Gospel to bear upon the mores, practices, customs, and laws of our society. We are called as Catholics, as followers of Jesus to use our God-given talents and abilities to make a difference in the world, to help our society to become more Christ-like in its culture, in its way of operating, in its values. We are called to build a **culture of life.**[155]

Our Church does not apologize for her public stance on the life issues, and no Catholic should feel intimated by the rhetoric and tactics of the other side. We must continue to speak out for the truth and for those who have no voice with which to influence the political process.

Good stewardship of the gift of human life does not permit us to settle for the declining standards of morality that permit the murder of innocent human beings in numbers that far outpace the atrocities of Hitler and Stalin combined.

Yes, we have lost this battle with the Food and Drug Administration, but we must not permit discouragement to

154 Matthew 28:19-20, emphasis added.
155 A phrase used often in the writings of Pope John Paul II.

cause us to lose the war. Rather, as Catholics, we must be **unambiguously pro-life** in our words and actions.[156] Let us be clear. In doing so we risk ridicule and the diminishment of our status in a society that is becoming increasingly a culture of death. May we be inspired and encouraged by the example and intercession of those holy martyrs down through the ages who gave up not popularity and status, but their very lives for the sake of the Kingdom of God.

Some things are more important than life or limb.

✠ **The Twenty-sixth Sunday in Ordinary Time (B)**
   October 1, 2000

Purgatory

Time is one of God's most precious gifts. The steward is conscious of the swiftness of the years, and the necessity to prepare for death. God's infinite mercy sustains the steward along life's journey, even through the purification known as purgatory.

There is much for us to think about as the autumn leaves pass their prime and begin to fall. Soon winter will be upon us in full force, the annual reminder that death comes for us all.

The Church invites us to ponder the mystery of death on a regular basis, especially during the month of November. The readings this day lead us in this direction. St. Paul tells us that when we grieve we do so not as the

---

[156] Physical or verbal violence to express one's opinion on life issues is never in keeping with the Gospel demand of charity.

pagans do, but as people who have hope in the saving death and resurrection of the Lord.[157] The Gospel presents the parable of the bridesmaids as a call to be prepared and as a sober reminder that **we know neither the day nor the hour.**[158]

In keeping with our tradition, **we pray for the dead,** asking the Lord to raise them up to glory. We entrust the souls of our loved ones to the tender mercies of a God who is always faithful to His promises, a gentle shepherd who leads His flock through the valley of the shadow of death into the land of verdant pastures and restful waters.[159]

We pray for the dead because our faith tells us that entrance into heaven is not automatic. Those who speak glibly about all the dead being in a better place are not speaking in conformity with the Scriptures. The Bible tells us that **salvation (heaven) is possible only through the death and resurrection of Jesus Christ.** The Bible also tells us that our actions here on earth have eternal consequences. Furthermore, we struggle with the effects of original sin throughout our lives. We get sidetracked. We lose our focus. We forget who we are.

Heaven is not automatic. Those who are in a persistent state of mortal sin when they die risk the flames of hell, eternal separation from God. To die without accepting God's merciful love is to be separated from Him by one's own free choice.[160] Only those who are pure and unblemished will enter heaven.[161] Only those who are in perfect communion with Christ Jesus are admitted into heaven.[162]

---

157 Cf. I Thessalonians 4:13,14.
158 Cf. Matthew 25:1-13.
159 Cf. Psalm 23.
160 Cf. CCC 1033-1036.
161 Cf. Revelation 21:27.
162 Cf. CCC 1026.

So where does that leave us poor sinners? Many of us will die with no unforgiven mortal sins on our souls, but few of us will die with our souls pure enough to enter heaven. Where does that leave us?

The Bible speaks of a cleansing fire which in the tradition of the Church is called *purgatory.* [163] It awaits those who die in a state of grace, but who are still imperfect. This cleansing fire is not at all like the fire of hell. Hell is about our rejection of God; purgatory is about the fire of God's love for us. Hell is eternal, but the cleansing fire of purgatory affects the soul only as long as is necessary to accomplish purification. *This fire is medicinal,* like the sting of alcohol on a wound. It is painful, but necessary for the process of healing. *This fire is like the bright sunlight* that hits the eyes of someone who has just walked out of a deep and dark cave.

In fact the analogy is a good one. We live out our lives in shadows of our own making, a very dim existence compared with the brightness of heaven's glory. When we die and step into God's light, it is going to hurt! We are going to be conscious of all those times we have turned away from God in this life. We will think about and be embarrassed by our poor stewardship: the missed opportunities, the energy we spent on things that were not at all important, and the laziness we showed in our relationship with God.

The time a person spends in purgatory may be long or short, depending upon how acclimated during life his or her eyes were to the light of God. Although God alone knows the state of the human soul, it is a pretty good bet that Mother Teresa probably slid through purgatory with ease, so close was she in this world to the light of Jesus Christ.[164] On

---

[163] Cf. 1Corinthians 3:10-15; I Peter 1:7; *purgatory* is from the Latin word *purgare:* to cleanse thoroughly from within.
[164] She was beatified less than one year after this homily was given.

the other hand, the person who lives a long life of sin and repents only on his deathbed will be spared the pains of hell, but he might have a long time to spend in the cleansing, purifying fire of purgatory.

That man and *all the souls in purgatory are helped by our prayers.* When we are in solidarity with them, when they know our love through the prayers we express, they are better able to accept the love of God that is the cleansing agent in purgatory.

We rightly pray for the dead, and we hope that others will remember us at the altar when we are gone from this life.

We are taught to pray for the dead by the Bible. Recall the account of Judas Maccabeus offering sacrifices at the Temple for his fallen comrades.[165]

We are taught to pray for the dead by the ancient tradition of the Church. Remember the words of the dying St. Monica to her son, St. Augustine: "One thing only I ask you, that you remember me at the altar of the Lord wherever you may be."[166]

And we are taught to pray for the dead by our forebears in the faith. I know of one faithful Catholic woman who gathered her children together when she knew that her days were numbered. In planning with them for her own funeral she stated sternly, "Don't even think about getting in the pulpit and making me out to be a saint. Don't canonize me with a flowery eulogy. Those words will do me no good. Instead, pray that the Lord might be merciful in judging my soul and that I might quickly pass through purgatory into the glory of heaven."

---

[165] Cf. II Maccabees 12:39-45.
[166] From *Confessions* by Saint Augustine, quoted in the Office of Readings for the Feast of Saint Monica.

On this November day, as the leaves fall and the wind blows ever colder, may we be conscious of our own mortality. May we "keep the flame of faith alive in [our hearts so that] when the Lord comes [we] might go out to meet Him with all the saints in the heavenly kingdom."[167] And may we never cease praising God for His great mercy. After all, **the doctrine of purgatory is all about God's abundant mercy.** God is so good to us. He so wants us to be with Him for all eternity that He gives us in this life chance after chance to do better. Even after death He gives us the purifying fires of purgatory so that our souls might be made perfect, ready to live in the glory of heaven for all eternity.

As we partake of the Holy Eucharist today, as we are nourished by the Lord Jesus, Body and Blood, Soul and Divinity, may we remember that our Holy Communion here is but **a foretaste of the everlasting banquet** of heaven. May this Sacrament strengthen us to keep our eyes fixed on faith's goal, our salvation.

✠ **The Thirty-second Sunday in Ordinary Time (A)**
November 10, 2002

---

[167] *The Rite of Baptism for Children,* p 60, # 1000.

CHAPTER FOUR:
THE MISSION OF THE STEWARD

"Go in peace, the Mass is ended" is much more than a call to clear the parking lot to get ready for the next Mass! It is a solemn charge to "go" and bring others to the great gift of the Lord Jesus received through the Holy Sacrifice of the Mass. The steward becomes more like the Lord through the reception of His Body and Blood; the steward's mission in life is to share that same Lord with others, thereby evangelizing the culture.

✠

The Virtues

Stewardship of Time means putting one's priorities in order, and attending to the most important things first. A good steward uses family time wisely, and in so doing makes an invaluable contribution to our Church and our world.

Christmas is the celebration of the mystery of the perfect communion of God, Father, Son and Holy Spirit as revealed in the context of the Holy Family. We do well to reflect on this feast day as to how "the Christian family ... is a community of faith, hope, and charity, [and how] it assumes singular importance in the Church."[168]

The family is especially well suited for education in the virtues. The family is a place where parents as well as children grow in the virtues and in so doing make an invaluable contribution to our Church and the wider society.

---

[168] CCC 2204.

123

However, *this growth in virtue is not automatic.* Allow me to illustrate:

Most of us as children participated in sports or music. In so doing we fell under the tutelage of a coach or teacher. We needed a coach or teacher because in spite of whatever natural abilities we brought to the sport or instrument we still had something to learn. In sports and music there are particular skills and abilities that need to be developed in practice so as to excel during the game or recital. Regardless of our natural talents we need the coach or teacher to help us to do the best we can do.

The same is true in life. *The particular skills we need to excel in life are called the virtues.* The human virtues make it possible for us to be at ease in doing the good. Just as mastery of the fundamentals allows an athlete to play with confidence and ease, and just as mastery of scales and techniques allows a musician to become a *virtuoso*, so does progress in the virtues allow us to be happy in the practice of the good.

In classical language, *the chief or cardinal virtues are four in number:*

- *prudence,* the foresight to see the consequences of actions and to act accordingly;
- *fortitude,* the inner strength to do what is right;
- *temperance,* the mastery of one's appetites; and
- *justice,* being in a state of right relations with others and with God.

When we acquire these virtues, we succeed in life (in the finest sense of the word *success*) for "the goal of a virtuous life is to become like God,"[169] the model and exemplar of virtuous living.

---

[169] CCC 1803, quoting St. Gregory of Nyssa, *De beatitudinibus*, 1: PG 44, 1200D.

Just as in athletics and music, we grow in the virtues by practice – by deliberate effort on our part, and by the grace of God that purifies and elevates our efforts. Parents as well as children find in the family *a place where the virtues can be exercised and developed.* As the gymnasium is to the athlete, and as the studio is to the musician, so the family is to the virtuous man or woman, boy or girl. In the family, in the give and take between brother and sister, parents and children, and in *an atmosphere* of "tenderness, forgiveness, respect, fidelity and [selfless] service"[170] a person can grow and develop in prudence, fortitude, temperance and justice, and thereby become more and more the person he or she was created to be.

However, we must not be naïve in thinking that growth in the virtues takes place automatically.

Imagine visiting your daughter's basketball practice. Imagine hearing the coach say to your daughter's team: "Tonight during practice you are free to do what you want to do. Here's the basketball, there's the hoop, now go out and have some fun doing what you want to do." I would bet that the coach would get an earful from you! And rightly so! Your daughter has so much to learn about basketball and so many skills to develop. This practice would be a waste of her valuable time. Furthermore, if this was the philosophy of coaching and every practice was a free-for-all, it would be a good bet that the team would fare miserably on game day. You would rightly be outraged.

Now, if it is the case that a negligent or apathetic basketball coach would get an earful from parents, then I hope that we are equally outraged at many of those who are coaching the virtues these days. Who are the negligent coaches of the virtues? Where do our children learn right from wrong? Too often the sanctuary of the family is violated through that which comes across the television

---

[170] CCC 2223.

screen. Too often we and our children are influenced by proponents of moral relativism and indifference to God. Too often we and our children are swayed by reports of polling data on important questions of morals and ethics. We and our children can be lulled into forgetting that polls measure changing feelings, but they do not measure steadfast principles.

I will save the diatribe against Hollywood and Washington D.C. for another day. But I do want to emphasize that the family is the privileged place for education in the virtues. What parents can teach their children, and (in many cases) what parents can learn from their children is absolutely priceless.

Because we seek to grow in the virtues, and because we hope that our children will grow in the virtues, I will suggest two things for all of us: ***Find a good coach,*** and ***practice, practice, practice!"***

To find a good coach in the virtues, look no farther than to the Child in the manger. He was born to teach us how to live. We do well to heed His words and to follow His example. And, we do well to remember that Jesus instituted the Church to continue His mission of teaching or coaching the virtues. Our Church articulates a beautiful and challenging moral vision.

Admittedly, parts of our Church's teaching are hard for some of us to follow. We might be tempted to pretend that those teachings do not apply to us. We might say that the Church's position on certain moral issues is too demanding, and that the Church should "lighten up." Yet just as a good coach always has a reason for the discipline and the high standards, so too with the Church. ***The motivation for the Church's moral teaching*** is a vision of who we are called to be as sons and daughters of God. And the goal of the Church's moral teaching is of vastly greater significance than that of any game. The goal is eternal life.

Practice, practice, practice! We learn from our own mistakes, and if we are fortunate we learn from the mistakes of others. "It is not easy ... to maintain moral balance [in life]."[171] We do well to pray for the grace Jesus offers us as we pursue growth in the virtues, for His grace gives us the strength to do good and to avoid evil. And we do well to ***frequent the sacraments***, especially Penance and the Eucharist, for in the sacraments does the Lord give us a share in His own life. By doing so, we avail ourselves of the opportunities for an increase in the grace of the Holy Spirit, a grace so vital to persevering in the virtues.

May our families be blessed this Christmas season. Through the intercession of the Blessed Mother and Saint Joseph, and through the power of our Lord and Savior Jesus Christ may we grow stronger in virtue and better reflect the love of the Holy Family in our daily living.

✠ **The Feast of the Holy Family (A)**
December 27, 1998

The Importance of Chastity

Stewardship of God's gift of the human body means exercising responsibility for the gift of sexuality, especially within the marriage covenant. Good stewards change the world by bearing witness to the truth about God's plan for marriage and family life.

I will give you as light to the nations", God promises the people of Israel through the prophet Isaiah, "that my salvation may reach to the end of the earth."[172]

What God says to Isaiah is exactly the same thing that He says to each and every one of us on our baptismal day. By

---

[171] CCC 1811.
[172] Isaiah 49:6.

configuring us to Christ Jesus, God makes us a light to the nations. By calling us to be followers of His Son, **God gives us a job to do: to be bearers of His light** so that the world might know His salvation.

The world is in desperate need of this light. As advanced and as sophisticated as our world is, there exist today shadows of darkness, areas of great ignorance that seem to extend bit by bit with every passing day. Sadly, our world has grown accustomed to this darkness and finds it difficult to recall the brilliance and splendor of the light.

I speak today of **a particular darkness: the widespread ignorance of the dignity of the human person** as created in the image and likeness of God. This ignorance manifests itself in the declining standards of morality and in ongoing violence against the most vulnerable members of our human family, the unborn and the dying.

In stark contrast to this darkness are those faithful stewards who serve as "bearers of the light", those who bring to bear the light of truth, the light of the Gospel through their daily living.

We live in **a culture that has forgotten about the importance of chastity before marriage**, the importance of waiting until sacred promises are made before the altar of God. **In contrast,** many teenagers and high school students pledge to do just that: to wait until marriage. They are not only making their personal pledge, they are acting as role models for younger teens. They tell others that **it's OK to wait** and that in searching for a life partner in marriage it is very important to find someone who will show the deepest respect for one's commitment to chastity. **Bearers of the light these young people are.**

We live in **a culture that has forgotten about the importance of chastity within marriage**, the importance of couples respecting their own fertility and using only those means of family planning that are in accord with God's laws.

In contrast, we have an increasing number of couples who are learning about the beauty and effectiveness of Natural Family Planning (NFP) and in so doing they find their own marriages enriched. In fact, many Saturday mornings, NFP classes are taught here courtesy of the Couple to Couple League. *Bearers of the light these couples are.*

We live in *a culture that has genuflected to the rhetoric of choice,* cloaking the brutal reality of abortion in the insidious language of "reproductive health". *In contrast,* there stands an army ready to march on Washington this Friday,[173] armed only with the weapons of prayer and the willingness to brave the January cold to engage in peaceable assembly. And behind the front lines of the Pro-Life Movement there thrives a vast network of resources for those who seek alternatives to abortion and for those who seek healing and reconciliation after experiencing the tragedy of abortion. No one is turned away and no one is scorned, praise God. *Bearers of the light these participants in the pro-life movement are.*

"I will make you a light to the nations," God tells us,[174] even as we dwell in a world marked by the *darkness of ignorance* about the dignity of the human person.

Each and every one of us is called to bear witness. We are to testify to the light of God's truth in the practice of the virtue of chastity and in our defense of the rights of the most vulnerable members of our human family, the unborn and the dying.

But let us be clear: we cannot bear the light of God's truth unless *we draw near to the source of that light.* If we try to change the world on our own we are doomed to failure. Our witness will be ineffective. Our voices will not

---

[173] For the annual March for Life, the anniversary of the *Roe v Wade* decision.

[174] Cf. Isaiah 49:6.

be heard. *Only when we draw close to the Lord, especially in prayer and the sacraments, can He can truly work within us.* When we are open to the Lord Jesus, allowing Him to touch and move our hearts, *then* we are able to bring His light to bear in our troubled world.

Bearers of the light. Good and faithful stewards – that is what we are called to be. That is what we are capable of being. That is what God created us to be. May we be keenly aware of the *nobility* of that calling.

May we discipline ourselves to pray, regularly taking the opportunity to open our hearts to the Lord Jesus, the Light of the world. Many people find it helpful to pray before the Blessed Sacrament, especially in the Adoration Chapel. The Blessed Sacrament exposed in the monstrance resembles the sun, for the Blessed Sacrament radiates the *light* of God's truth and the *warmth* of God's love.

May we draw near to that light and that warmth, not simply for our own sake, but for the sake of a world that dwells in the darkness of ignorance. For it is a darkness that can be overcome only when we act as bearers of God's light.

✠ **The Second Sunday in Ordinary Time (A)**
January 17, 1999

Faith Compartmentalized

The practice of stewardship effects in a person an integration of the material and the spiritual dimensions of his or her life. Stewardship is a remedy for the disintegration of the person brought about by the compartmentalization of faith.

The Good Samaritan has long been an image of Christian charity.[175] Those who stop to offer assistance to the

---

[175] Luke 10:29-37.

stranger in need are called "Good Samaritans," even by those who do not share our faith.

In fact, **the Good Samaritan is an image of Jesus Christ Himself,** the author of Christian charity. The man in the ditch represents humanity, robbed of its dignity by sin, left half-dead by the treachery of the devil. The priest and the Levite represent the Old Law, unable to save humanity from eternal peril. The Good Samaritan is Jesus, who enters the world in order to rescue the fallen human race, paying the price not with silver coins, but literally with His blood, rising on the third day to complete His work of redemption.

Jesus, the Good Samaritan, graciously rescues us from our base desires, heals us of our sin, and raises us up to new life. And, as we learn through our practice of stewardship, what we have received we are called to share with others through Christian charity, the works of compassion and mercy.

Charity, in fact has always been the defining quality of a Christian. The Christian is recognized not by a distinctive garb, but by his or her love.[176] It is by the power of the Holy Spirit that we have the love of Christ in our hearts. We are equipped to love as Christ loves, as exemplified in the parable of the Good Samaritan.

Let's go a step further with this parable of the Good Samaritan. I'm going to make a guess about the priest and the Levite in the parable. I'm going to guess that as each of them passed the man in the ditch they each said a prayer for him. They were, after all, very religious men.

And, I'll guess that when they reached their destination they shook their heads and complained to all their friends about how dangerous it is on the road between Jerusalem and Jericho, and how it wasn't that way when they were growing

---

[176] Cf. *A Letter to Diognetus,* The Office of Readings, Wednesday of the Fifth Week of Easter.

up. "Surely the man in the ditch is just one more sign of the decline of society and the collapse of civilization," they said, eloquently and convincingly.

What was the matter with the priest and the Levite, these two intelligent, religious men? What kept them from stopping to help the man in the ditch? What prompted them to **cross to the other side of the road** when they saw that poor man?

They had compartmentalized their faith. They were religious men, but their faith was kept in a compartment, as it were, isolated from their daily living. They had faith, but they were content allowing their faith to remain a personal matter, distant and aloof from every day life.

Jesus is very clear about this "compartmentalized faith" of the priest and the Levite. He says that **it doesn't cut it.** It just won't do: "How can you say you love the God you cannot see if you do not show concern for the neighbor you do see?"[177] "Faith without works is dead."[178] Our faith in Jesus Christ is a precious gift, a gift that moth and rust cannot destroy nor can thief or brigand carry away.[179] But our faith is not meant to be kept within. It is meant to be shared, to be put into action.

How do we apply this parable of the Good Samaritan in our daily lives? Here are but three examples:

Let's begin with our families, where the culture of death clutches our children through the tentacles of the entertainment industry, an industry that shows blatant and defiant disrespect for God's gift of sexuality and the family. We have a choice. We can ignore the undesirable influence of TV and movies on our children. We can **cross to the other side of the street** as it were and pretend not to notice. **Or we can confront it,** offering our children guidance and

---

[177] Cf. 1 John 4:20.
[178] Cf. James 2:17.
[179] Cf. Matthew 6:19, 20.

direction that is protested against, but nonetheless is deeply needed and wanted.

Let's branch out to the wider community, even here at the parish, where gossip and rumor mongering lay waste to many a reputation. We can ignore the gossip and *cross to the other side of the street,* pretending not to notice. *Or we can confront it,* asking the gossip direct questions such as "How do you know for sure?" "Is that the whole story?" "What proof do you have?" Direct questions have deflated many a dangerous rumor.

Finally, *let's apply this parable of the Good Samaritan by bringing our faith to bear upon the issues of the day.* We can, for example, ignore the harvesting of embryos for stem cell research. We can pretend that life really doesn't begin at conception. We can *cross to the other side of the street* and pretend not to notice. *Or we can confront the issue* and make our voice heard, for under *no* circumstances is it permitted to destroy innocent human life, not even for potential medical progress. There must be another way to cure diseases such as cancer, Parkinson's and diabetes. And if there is no other way, then we must stand up and say that even one innocent life is far too great a price to pay. There are worse things, after all, than physical illness and death.

By the Spirit we are given the love of Jesus Christ; that love *needs to be nourished by the sacraments.* It is a love that seeks to penetrate every aspect of our lives. As we walk along the road of life, may we keep our eyes open to the opportunities we have to be good stewards and to make a difference, to bring the love of Jesus Christ into our world. May our sharing in the Lord's Body and Blood prevent us from ignoring the man in the ditch. *May our faith never be compartmentalized.*

✠ **The Fifteenth Sunday in Ordinary Time (C)**
July 15, 2001

The Difference We Can Make

The Holy Eucharist is the heart of the life of the Church, the source of our courage in confronting the culture of death. The Lord uses humble stewards to accomplish the up-building of His Kingdom. Christian stewards use all of their gifts and talents in the service of their Lord.

The needs of the people were considerable.[180] Evening was rapidly approaching; the people hadn't taken a break to eat all day. And the disciples of Jesus were worried.

They proposed to Jesus a solution: Send the people away and let them find something to eat. When Jesus counter-proposed that the disciples feed the people themselves, the disciples protested, "We have so little – hardly enough for ourselves – just five loaves and two fish!"[181]

The disciples were in the process of learning an invaluable lesson: even though what they had to give was seemingly very little, **with Jesus their resources were more than enough.**

It's a lesson that we need to be reminded of time and again. So often parents feel inadequate when they think about their children's needs as they grow up in this ever-changing world. "Am I being a good steward of God's gift of children? Am I providing for my children all that they need? Is what I have to give as a parent adequate? I feel so stretched – pulled from all directions. Am I giving enough?"

What parent doesn't feel at one time or another that he or she has seemingly little to give. Yet the Lord assures us that if we are with Him, and if we allow ourselves to be instruments of His peace and grace, **what little we have to give (our prayers, our presence, our love, our direction) will be more than enough.**

---

[180] Matthew 14:13-21.
[181] Cf. Matthew 14:17.

So often, too, as citizens we feel inadequate when we think about the society in which we live. A society in which kids kill kids, in which a disgruntled investor goes on a murderous rampage, and in our own neighborhood a very disgruntled driver crashes through the entrance of a hospital. In what kind of society are we living when these incidents make the headlines, but the silent holocaust against the unborn continues day after day, amassing casualties that number nearly 1.5 million per year in this country alone?

What is to be our stance as Christians in our society today? **What do we have to give that will make a difference?** Seemingly very little. It's a hopeless case we might say. But the Lord wants to assure us today that if we are united with Him, what little we have to give – our prayer, our witness, our commitment to truth, our faithful stewardship – will be more than enough and will, in fact, make a considerable difference in this troubled world of ours.

For just as Jesus transformed five loaves and two fish into a banquet that fed a multitude, so does Jesus work through us. **Weak and limited though we are, He does on earth the work He wants to accomplish.** As expressed so beautifully in words often ascribed to St. Teresa of Avila: "Christ has no body now on earth but yours. No hands but yours. No feet but yours. Yours are the eyes through which the compassion of Christ must look out on the world. Yours are the feet with which He is to go about doing good. Yours are the hands with which He is to bless His people."

Jesus works through us to accomplish His work on earth. That is the important lesson. Each time the Mass is offered, Jesus reinforces the lesson by accepting the gifts we present, the simple bread and the common table wine, gifts that represent all that we have to offer our Lord. Through the priest, Our Lord takes these gifts, blesses them, and shares them with us, but not unchanged. We give Him bread and wine worth but a few pennies and He gives us the precious gift of His Body and Blood, the gift that is worth far *more than silver or gold.*[182]

The gift of the Eucharist is a reminder that Jesus takes what little we have and refashions it into that which builds the Kingdom of God. Jesus gives us the Eucharist so that He can be within us to strengthen us as we strive to accomplish His will for our troubled world.

If we wonder whether we have what it takes to give our children what they need, may we remember the lesson of this Gospel: *though what we have may be seemingly little, with Jesus it is more than enough.* If we wonder if we can make a difference in this culture of death, may we stay close to Jesus, especially through the Sacrament of the Eucharist. May He amplify the seemingly little that we have and make of our stewardship something that truly builds up the Kingdom of God.

✠ **The Eighteenth Sunday in Ordinary Time (A)**
August 1, 1999

In Defense of Chastity

The virtue of chastity is nothing less than stewardship of the body for the service of love and life and the building up of the Kingdom of God. Though often forgotten these days, chastity is a virtue at the service of human relationships.

At the very heart of the teaching of Jesus Christ is a personal call to live in a manner befitting our human dignity. In the Gospels, *Jesus calls us to purity of heart.* That call to holiness and purity "raises the bar" of expectations and challenges us to go beyond the world's mores. Jesus challenges us because He believes in us and

---

[182] Cf. 1 Peter 1:18, 19.

because He promises the gifts and graces of the Holy Spirit that enable us to live out our Christian calling.

The human body – indeed, the human person – is a beautiful creation of God. God reveals His mind and heart in creating man and woman in His own image and likeness. In fact, God shares with man and woman the ability to imitate His own love and to participate in the work of creation. We are called to be stewards of the gift of life and love. This is why our human sexuality must never be defined just biologically, that is merely as a reproductive system. Rather, through our God-given sexuality, our bodies are integrated with our spirits. *God designed man and woman so that the way in which they express tenderness, intimacy and unity would be the very way in which new life would be brought into the world.* Because God designed it so, we can join in God's own assessment of His creation and say, "It is good – in fact, it is very good!"[183]

If this is so, how is it that so much ugliness is associated with sexuality? How is it that sexuality is all too often the subject of "dirty jokes," tawdry television talk shows, and the reporting of public scandals involving "inappropriate relationships"?

How is it that we experience difficulties in keeping the Sixth and Ninth Commandments, especially as Jesus has interpreted them? Remember, Jesus says, "You have heard that it was said, 'You shall not commit adultery.' But I say to you that every one who looks at [another] lustfully has already committed adultery [in the heart]."[184]

Good people certainly fall short at times in the practice of the virtue of chastity. As chastity is too often forgotten altogether these days, marriages and family become even

---

[183] Cf. Genesis 1:31.
[184] Matthew 5:27-28.

more vulnerable. Consequently, *as marriage and family life are weakened, our society is at grave risk.*[185]

Chastity is not prudishness nor is it a puritanical rejection of things pleasurable. *Chastity is a virtue at the service of human relationships,* and, as such, can never be simply a "private matter." The practice of chastity affects the bonds of the entire human family.

Chastity is the God-given inclination or disposition to control our passions and to integrate our sexuality into all aspects of our persons. It brings self-mastery so that we might enter into relationships with others that are healthy, virtuous, and respectful of others God-given dignity.[186] *Chastity is a gift ordered toward the integration* (as opposed to the compartmentalization) of our person, our actions, and our desires.[187]

What is a chaste person like? Far from being uptight or square the person who practices chastity finds *happiness* in the practice of virtue.

We see this *happiness in the married couple* whose devotion and love for one another is accompanied by an openness to God's will for their fertility. That couple's chaste love for one another bears witness to the unconditional love of Jesus for his people, the Church.

We see this *happiness in single people* in whom "the virtue of chastity blossoms in friendship."[188] They maintain in their persons "the integrity of the powers of life and love."[189] Furthermore, chastity practiced in dating and in the time of

---

Cf. CCC 2207.
[186] Cf. CCC 2339
[187] Cf. CCC 2337, 2338.
[188] CCC 2347
[189] CCC 2338.

engagement tends to lead to a stronger, more loving marriage.[190]

We see this *happiness in those who profess chastity as a vow* or way of life as part of their religious or priestly calling. The chastity of the priest or religious leads that person into a deeper relationship with God, who is Love, and provides the world a witness to the abiding love of Jesus.[191]

At the very heart of the teaching of Jesus Christ is a personal call to live in a manner befitting our human dignity. Pope John Paul II has reminded us, "Love is the fundamental and innate vocation [calling] of every human being."[192] *Chastity is at the service of love and life.*

Chastity is a personal matter – for it is up to each of us to strive for purity of heart in our discourse, our entertainments, and our relationships. While *personal*, chastity is more than a *private* matter, for it profoundly impacts the health and well being of our society.

Let us then avail ourselves of the opportunities for closeness with person of Jesus Christ, the model of chastity, the one in whom Love is made flesh. *Let us turn to Him in the Sacrament of Penance* for forgiveness for our sins against chastity, and let us receive from Him the grace we need to grow in virtue and holiness. *Let us be nourished with His Body and Blood* so that our eyes might be opened to see the human body – ours and our neighbor's – as a temple of the Holy Spirit, a manifestation of divine beauty. May we always seek the intercession of our Blessed Mother, model of purity and virtue.

✠ **The Twenty-first Sunday in Ordinary Time (C)**
   August 23, 1998

---

[190] Many divorce statistics bear this out. For further information see the pastoral statement issued by the Bishops of Pennsylvania at www.pacatholic.org
[191] Cf. CCC 916.
[192] Pope John Paul II in *Familiaris consortio*, 11, quoted in CCC 2392.

God's Will: *Just Do It*

In order to do his job well, a steward must know the will of the owner. The practice of stewardship entails a lifetime of striving to know the will of God and, with the help of His grace, to put God's will into practice. The good steward "walks the talk."

This parable of the vineyard owner's sons[193] is easy to understand, but challenging to live by. The father in the parable makes his expectations known to his two sons. Which of the two does the father's will? The one who, though initially defiant, changes his mind and goes about his father's business.

It's all very simple, isn't it? *Just do it.* Just do the will of our heavenly Father, and all will be well.

A wise person seeks **to know God's will.** Another term for the **will** of God is the **plan** of God. In fact, it is not difficult to know God's plan for our lives. We need only to **open the Bible** to discover what God tells us to do if we are to find happiness in this world and eternal life in the world to come. When a person is open to understanding the Bible and the teachings of our Catholic Church, that person has a pretty good sense of God's will for his or her life.

What about when it comes to the details, such as "Is this the person to whom I should propose?" or "What is the best approach for solving this family problem?" We learn throughout our lives that **there is no substitute for prayer.** When we pray regularly and faithfully we learn more and more about God's will for the particulars of our lives. Make no mistake about it, God doesn't speak in a booming voice — at least He hasn't to me! But He gives plenty of gentle nudges if we are prayerful enough to notice.

---

[193] Matthew 21:28-32.

To know God's will is the first step toward the good life, the life of walking with God as a true follower and making a positive difference in our world. For example: we know that marriage and family are the building blocks of our Church, our nation and our civilization. When marriages and families start to crumble, our civilization goes into a downward spiral.

That being said, ***how can a person know God's will*** as a father or mother, a husband or wife, if he or she is not paying attention to the Word of God contained in the Bible? ***How can a married person know God's will*** if he or she is not paying attention to the teachings of the Church? If a person's mind and heart are closed to the wisdom of the Church pertaining to fidelity, openness to children, and the proper means of family planning, how can that person ever hope to follow God's plan, God's direction?

If ***an engaged couple*** dismisses the Church's teaching on cohabitation as being irrelevant to this day and age, how can that couple ever hope to find the happiness God has in store for them? ***When a single person*** says that Jesus' teaching on chastity is too difficult or that the Lord is "out of touch" with life in the third millennium, how can that person ever hope to find the spouse God intends?

And if ***a person considering the priesthood or religious life*** is not disciplined while discerning the call, but allows distractions to rule his or her life, how can that person ever hope to know the path the Lord has in mind?

To know God's will requires of us an open mind: openness to the rock-solid teachings of the Bible and the time-tested wisdom of the Church. And ***it requires prayer.*** The quiet and communication developed in a regular prayer life enable us to hear more readily what the Lord speaks in the sanctuary of our hearts.

Knowing God's will is the first step. **The second** is very simple: as the Nike advertisements says, **Just do it.**

How does one **just do it?** By living a disciplined life. To **just do it** as an athlete, one follows a strict program of training and diet. To **just do it** as a disciple of Jesus one must be **disciplined** in exercising the virtues. In fact, the words are from similar Latin roots. The Christian disciple exercises the virtues by repeatedly showing courage in the face of ridicule, by persevering in times of difficulty, and by being strong in dealing with temptations.

To be a disciple also requires one to **be nourished regularly by the sacraments of the Church,** especially the Sacraments of Penance and the Holy Eucharist. **In Penance** we find forgiveness of our sins and the grace of new life that comes directly from the cross of Jesus.

And **in the Holy Eucharist** we find the grace and strength that comes from sharing in the Lord's Body and Blood, Soul and Divinity, that inexhaustible source of spiritual comfort and edification that allows us to:

- **put into practice the faith we profess;**
- **walk the talk; and**
- **Just do it.**

May we seek the grace of God made available to us in the sacraments. May we resolve to make time for the quiet that is so necessary in listening to the Lord's direction in our lives, to sense those gentle nudges that reveal His will, His plan. And, in Him, may each of us find the strength and wisdom to **"Just do it."**

✠ **The Twenty-sixth Sunday in Ordinary Time (A)**
September 29, 2002

Culture of Death, Culture of Life

The parable of the "dishonest" steward provides the opportunity to consider the stewardship of human life. This homily was preached less than two weeks after September 11, 2001. Like the steward in the Gospel, we are called to the deepest respect for the treasure of the Master, in this case, the lives of the unborn.

In today's Gospel, St. Luke introduces us to a steward to whom much has been entrusted by his master.[194] *Much is expected of the one to whom much has been entrusted,*[195] but this steward squanders his master's resources instead. Rather than investing wisely, he wastes resources that are not his own to do with as he pleases. He forgets that he is not the owner of these goods, but that he is only their steward.

And then, out of the blue, he is asked for an account of his stewardship. He is given a wake-up call that he will never forget. His network of lies comes crashing down. Instantaneously, the frivolous, wasteful steward undergoes a conversion. He becomes shrewd and ingenious. He cuts his losses. "To dig I am unable, to beg I too proud,"[196] he says, and so he makes things right in a way that gains the admiration of his master. Instead of dismissing the steward, the master gives him a second chance.

How does this parable apply to us?

Just as much was entrusted to that steward, so too has much been entrusted to our nation. Our founding fathers had a profound sense of the great blessings and the

---

[194] Luke 16:1-13. This parable of the clever steward is a difficult one. With the opportunity of an hour-long Scripture study, I might be able to blaze a trail through some of its more obscure images. Suffice it to say that this passage refers to an ancient Semitic culture, largely unfamiliar to us. Another discussion for another time!

[195] Cf. Luke 12:48.

[196] Cf. Luke 16:3.

marvelous opportunities that God had given to our fledgling country. Unshackled from the tyranny of a monarchy, the new republic would flourish under a constitution that guarantees the security of the inalienable, God-given rights of life, liberty and the pursuit of happiness. To this day we enjoy material prosperity and personal freedom that is the envy of the world. God has given so much to us. *So much has been entrusted to us to be used wisely and prudently, to be cherished and shared so as to give glory and honor to God.*

And yet, like the steward in the Gospel, we seem to forget that we are *only* stewards. The blessings of life and liberty are not ours to do with as we please. As part of God's providence and design, they are entrusted to us to be cherished and used wisely, to accomplish God's purpose. That sentiment should pervade our national consciousness at every hour. Much has been given to us, and much is expected in return. We've forgotten that, haven't we? We've grown lax as a nation. We've worshipped the false idols of materialism, secularism, and hedonism. *We've turned our backs on our partnership with God.*

We've made an illicit claim to be able to do as we please with the blessings of life and liberty, by insisting, for example, that we have the right to choose whether an unborn baby lives or dies. And if we, the most blessed nation on earth, can accept without flinching the deliberate, legally-sanctioned killing of the unborn, the defenseless in the womb, how can we expect those not of our culture to desist from the despicable crime of terrorism, the killing of defenseless non-combatants? If we value the assertion of choice more than innocent human life, how can we expect those not of our culture to value human life more than the desire to assert a political stance through terrorism?

We have experienced firsthand the implications of the culture of death. *We are called to cooperate with God in bringing forth a culture of life.*

Perhaps the ultimate good that God brings forth from the evil of September 11 is a wake-up call for our nation. Perhaps the events of that terrible day will effect a great conversion within us: a change in our national consciousness. From the darkness there could emerge a reawakened conviction about the sanctity of human life.

The brave rescue teams at the World Trade Center know far better than any of us that *human life is not a commodity, but a precious gift from God* that we often take for granted until it is too late. The heroism of ordinary people on September 11 reveals that there is within each of us a deeply-rooted conviction about the dignity of every human person. Men and women will place themselves in harm's way to save lives, and they will do it at a moment's notice, without counting the cost.

For me, this is proof positive that the choice for life is of an infinitely higher order than the so-called right to choose. The former shows what is the very best of our human nature; the latter reveals a corruption of that which is good.

We stand united as a nation against the evils of terrorism. We cherish our way of life too dearly to ever let terror win the day. Please God, may our zeal against terrorism be translated into a fervent desire to extend the protection of our constitution to *all innocent human life from the moment of conception until natural death.*

Like the steward in the Gospel, may we see in the wake-up call of September 11 an opportunity to get our affairs in order, to realign our priorities, and to remember that our Creator has endowed every human person, born and unborn, with certain inalienable rights, and among them is the right to life.

✠ **The Twenty-fifth Sunday in Ordinary Time (C)**
September 23, 2001

Stewardship of Human Life

Stewardship means exercising responsibility for the gift of human life: our own, our children, those who have no voice. In our day, stewardship entails a firm commitment to the pro-life movement.

Over these past few weeks, we have learned a number of things about stewardship: **stewardship is a way of life** marked by **thankfulness, responsibility and generosity** – summed up in a genuine **attitude of gratitude** for all of God's blessings. We are called to live out our awareness that we are not owners of God's creation. God is the owner. We are the caretakers, the managers, **the stewards.** We give glory and honor to God by the quality of our stewardship.

We've reflected upon the stewardship of time, talent, and treasure, but today I want to speak about a much more fundamental kind of stewardship – stewardship of the precious gift of human life.

The Scriptures today could not be any clearer about God bestowing the precious gift of human life. In the creation of Adam and Eve, God creates man and woman in His image and likeness,[197] in a complementary relationship. By God's design, man and woman are capable of entering into holy matrimony – the two becoming one body[198] for the sake of mutual, fruitful, committed love and so that children could be brought into the world through that love.

Human life is a magnanimous gift from God. **Every** human being is created in His image and likeness; each is unique, possessing an immortal soul, destined for eternal life with Him. Every human life is sacred – from the moment of conception until natural death.

---

[197] Cf. Genesis 1:26.
[198] Cf. Mark 10: 8; Ephesians 5:31.

Human life is a gift, a great gift and we are all stewards of that gift. We exercise that stewardship in *three ways:*

First, in a personal sense, we are called to be good stewards of the life God gives to each of us – our own life. We are called to take care of ourselves by eating right, staying active and fit, getting regular medical care, exercising moderation in the consumption of alcohol and tobacco, keeping our minds alert, reading good books, engaging in meaningful conversation, participating in entertainment that uplifts the soul.

Second, we are called to *stewardship of life in regard to others.* Parents are responsible for their children. Parents do not own their children, but they are stewards of the lives God has entrusted to them. Parents must attend to not only the physical and emotional well-being of their children, but also to their moral and spiritual formation as well.

Sometimes we are called to be good stewards of the lives of others who are in our care, such as a relative or an elderly parent unable to make independent decisions. In such circumstances, *we must always act in that person's best interest.* Period. And when there are tough questions to answer – matters of life and death – we must *seek the wisdom of the Church.* Please know that priests are always willing to spend time with you and your family during those times when difficult matters call for tough decisions.

Finally, we are called to *stewardship of life as members of a society.* We are blessed to live in a country in which our voices and our votes count. We all learned in the last two national elections[199] that *every vote counts.* That being the case, we have a particular obligation to pay attention to abuses of the gift of life, and to recognize the

---

[199] The 2000 and 2004 Presidential elections.

opportunity we have to speak out on behalf of those who have no voice of their own.

We must exercise our duty to be vigilant in the cause of life.

We must remain aware of the heinous violence against human life in the womb committed well over one million times every year in our country through the sin of abortion.

We must be aware that powerful forces in our country profit substantially from legalized abortion on demand, and spend ungodly sums of money to maintain its legality.

We must not turn a blind eye to the fact that these powerful forces have exercised a stranglehold on many labor unions and upon the political process. These forces will resist with all their might any attempt to restrict abortions – even the gruesome procedure known as partial birth abortion, a procedure done in the latest stage of pregnancy, a procedure that is medically unwarranted. According to medical experts, there is no circumstance when that procedure is the only way to save a mother's life.[200] Legislation to ban this reprehensible procedure has been passed and will soon be signed into law, thank God, but watch for the legal wrangling to follow. And look for the most aggressive campaign to be waged against

---

[200] "A select panel convened by ACOG could identify no circumstances under which this procedure ... would be the only option to save the life or preserve the health of the woman." American College of Obstetricians and Gynecologists *Statement of Policy,* January 12, 1997.

"The partial delivery of a living fetus for the purpose of killing it outside the womb is ethically offensive to most Americans and physicians. Our panel could not find any identified circumstance in which the procedure was the only safe and effective abortion method." AMA President Daniel Johnson Jr., MD, in the *New York Times,* May 26, 1997.

For additional information visit the Pro-life Activities section of the American bishops' website: www.usccb.org/prolife

judges who would show the slightest tendency to give back to the states the right to restrict or outlaw abortion (as was the case before the 1973 decision *Roe v Wade*).

We must be aware, alert, vigilant. Every vote counts. Every letter or phone call to an elected representative is duly noted. St. Vincent de Paul counseled, "Do the good you can do today." One person cannot do **everything**, but every person here can do **something** for the cause of the pro-life movement.

Here are some specific ways you can make a difference:

Participate actively in the political process, especially if the party of your choice is going down an evil path or if it is not sufficiently assertive in standing up for what is right. Make your voice known to those who are the movers and shakers in the world of politics, locally, statewide and nationally.

Become active in the pro-life movement. Volunteer to counsel those who think abortion is the only answer. Help to solicit contributions that make it possible for the movement to advertise its views and to thereby keep the issue in the forefront of people's minds.

If you are a teen or college-age parishioner, I would urge you to **be a good friend.** You are on the front line of the pro-life movement. A friend in trouble will speak with you long before speaking to a counselor or even a parent. Let that friend know that there are always alternatives to abortion – that there are loving couples eager to adopt, and that the Church stands ready to help in any way possible. **You are on the front lines of the pro-life movement.**

Last but not least, **pray.** There is great power in prayer. Prayer stopped the Turks at the gates of Vienna and brought victory at Lepanto. Prayer loosened the chains of the slaves and caused the Iron Curtain to fall without a single shot being fired. Prayer makes a difference. It is **the** most powerful weapon we have in our arsenal as we battle the greatest evil of our day. *There is no substitute for prayer; with God, nothing is impossible.*[201]

On this Respect Life Sunday, may we recommit ourselves to be good stewards of our lives and of every life that God has placed in our care. May we resolve to confront both the overt and subtle elements of the culture of death. May we draw our strength from the Holy Eucharist, that by the grace of this sacrament we might individually and collectively become better stewards of the gift of human life.

✠ **Twenty-seventh Sunday in Ordinary Time (B)**
October 5, 2003

---

[201] cf. Luke 1:37.

CHAPTER FIVE:
HOMILIES FOR THE
STEWARDSHIP SEASON

Stewardship is not a program, but it can and should be taught in a programmatic way. Every year my parish devotes about a month to ongoing stewardship education. During this month, parishioners learn about stewardship through bulletin inserts, mailings, lay witness talks during announcement time at Mass, and homilies from the pastor. The homilies that follow were preached during the season on ongoing stewardship education.

✠

Buried Treasure

God the Father is so good to us, especially in drawing us to Himself through the life, death, and resurrection of His Son, our Lord Jesus. He bestows upon us magnanimous spiritual treasures, compelling the good steward to invest in those same treasures wholeheartedly.

The search for buried treasure brings to mind images from the Indiana Jones movies: secret passages through caves, dangerous escapes, ancient maps where "X" marks the spot.

A man finds buried treasure in today's Gospel.[202] Though hardly as exciting as when Indiana Jones finds the treasure, the man in the Gospel makes a discovery that forever changes his life.

What are the circumstances of his unearthing of this treasure? As a matter of fact, he **stumbles** across it. From what is told in the Gospel story, he is probably a tenant

---

[202] Matthew 13:44-52.

farmer. Perhaps, while working in the fields, his plow hits an object embedded in the ground. From the sound the plow makes when it hits the object, the farmer thinks that it is something other than a rock. His curiosity gets the best of him and he begins to dig at the object with his hands.

His heart starts to race when he sees that it is an ornately decorated coffer. He remembers stories from his childhood of how families buried their treasures in fields in anticipation of the ransacking by conquering armies – and how many of those wealthy people never lived to reclaim their treasured coffers.

Lo and behold, the simple tenant farmer has stumbled across a treasure box filled with gems and gold worth far more than he could have ever imagined – enough to catapult his family across several class lines and secure not only his own future, but also that of his children and grandchildren.

Of course, he would sell everything he has to purchase the tract of land so the treasure would be legally his. One would have to be a fool not to make that kind of transaction. And having purchased the field, the tenant farmer and his lovely family live happily and luxuriously ever after on the fortuitous discovery.

And that, Jesus says, is like the Kingdom of God!

You see, God plants in each of our hearts a sense that **there is much more to life than meets the eye.** God puts in our souls an intuition that below the surface of our ordinary lives there lay mysterious treasures and hidden riches.

God gives each of us the inner sense that our lives have an infinitely profound meaning and purpose. Some refer to this inner sense as **an openness to the transcendent,** an openness to that which is beyond our senses. As Christians we understand this inner sense to be a sign of the existence of our soul, for we bear within "... the seed of eternity, which cannot be reduced to mere matter."[203]

We have an inner sense of the incredible treasure that rests beneath the surface. But **often we are completely oblivious** to the fact that we are standing so close to the riches that can profoundly change our lives.

But every so often we hear the plow strike the embedded object. The plow stops suddenly with a jolt, such as when our lives are interrupted by moments of tragedy or by moments of sheer grace (the teenager who tells the parents "I love you" at the moment they really need to hear those words). It is then that our inner sense is awakened and we begin **to dig – to question – to probe – to search** for that which is hidden beneath the surface of our everyday lives. We begin to look beyond the material world for answers. **We are led to that which cannot be measured in human terms,** but that which is infinitely good, infinitely valuable. **We are in fact led to God.** We discover that God is neither abstract nor distant, but that He is near – just below the surface of our ordinary existence.

God is the hidden treasure, the pearl of great price who is there all along just waiting for us to dig deep enough to find Him. The practice of good stewardship commits us to investing our lives in the good things of the Kingdom of Heaven. It means making concrete choices to prefer nothing to the love of Jesus Christ, the pearl of great price.

"The Kingdom of Heaven is like treasure hidden in a field, which a man found and covered up; then in his joy he goes and sells all that he has and buys that field."[204] And he lives happily ever after.

---

[203] *Gaudium et spes* 18 § 1.
[204] Matthew 13:44.

We are here in Church today either because we have found that buried treasure, or because we are still searching. In either case, *we offer thanks for the inner sense* that tells us that there is far more to life than meets the eye. We trust that the search for purpose, meaning, and immortality leads to the One who is the Way, the Truth, and the Life – the One who reveals to us the hidden treasures that lay just below the surface.

This is our faith in Jesus Christ. Following His sacred command we draw near to Him once more. *Within these walls, under this roof,* bread and wine are changed through the miracle of the Eucharist. To us is given a gift worth far *more than silver or gold* [205] – the priceless treasure of our Lord's Body and Blood. How blessed we are to be called to His supper, and to have found so near to us what many search for a lifetime to find. And having found the incredible riches of God's love in the Holy Eucharist, it is clear that *it is worth everything we have to possess that love more completely.* For how could we prefer anything else to the infinitely valuable treasure of God's love?

✠ **The Seventeenth Sunday in Ordinary Time (A)**
July 25, 1999

---

[205] Cf. 1 Peter 1:8.

Parenting as Stewardship

The responsibility and generosity shown by Christian parents is a beautiful example of stewardship: faith in action that reveals the love of the Lord.

During my sophomore year in college, everyone in my hallway pooled his funds to purchase a coffee maker. It was wonderful to be able to enjoy a cup of coffee at any hour of the day or night.

The coffee maker **belonged to everyone.** It was collective property. And as a result (sadly) it **belonged to no one.** You might remember the "ghosts" in the Family Circus cartoon – ghosts named **No one** and **Not me.** Those ghosts seemed to move into our hallway with the purchase of the coffee machine. Who cleaned it? **No one.** Who took care of it? **No one.** Whose responsibility was it? **Not me.** What started out to be so wonderful for all the coffee lovers lasted but a few weeks before the coffee maker was irreparably broken.

Had one person owned the coffee maker it would have lasted much longer. Alas, that piece of wisdom was lost on a group of idealistic college sophomores.

Ownership is virtuous because it instills a sense of responsibility and care. This is as true with college dormitory coffee makers as it is in economics. As we have learned from the experiences of this century, the economics of collectivism (socialism) provide fertile ground for the politics of tyranny and oppression (communism).

The lesson that **ownership and freedom go hand-in-hand** should never be forgotten.

But ownership is relative to a far greater reality. Who is the real owner of the earth and all its fullness? Who is the Master of the seas, the land, and all that is in them? Who else, but the Lord – the Almighty, the Creator and Sustainer of the Universe?

God owns everything! The sun, the sky, the land, the seas, everything! To us, His creatures, *He has entrusted the use of all these wonderful gifts.* To us, His creatures, He has endowed intangible gifts as well: creativity, ingenuity, fortitude, prudence – virtues that enable us to achieve, to accomplish, to attain. The very ability to earn a living and enjoy prosperity is itself a great gift from God.

Only in relationship to one another are we the owners of property. *In relationship to God we are not owners at all – but stewards.* A good steward is one who:

- *receives gifts gratefully from God;*
- *tends and cherishes those gifts responsibly;*
- *shares those gifts generously out of a sense of justice and love; and*
- *makes a return to the Lord with increase.* [206]

I know that hearing the word *stewardship* can send up red flags with some. After all, isn't stewardship just a ruse for talking about the Church's need for money?

I would like for us to think about **stewardship in a much broader sense.** In fact we can look at Christian parenthood as a beautiful example of stewardship.

Husband and wife enter into marriage promising to "accept children lovingly from God, and to bring them up according to the laws of Christ and His Church."[207]

The word "accept" has a rich connotation, for a child does not belong to his or her parents. *A child is entrusted*

[206] Cf. *Stewardship: A Disciple's Response: A Pastoral Letter on Stewardship,* United States Conference of Catholic Bishops, 1992.
[207] *The Rite of Marriage,* p. 12.

to them by God – to be educated, cared for, and raised in the practice of the faith.

Each child is unique. Each has individual gifts and talents, struggles and challenges. Every time a human life is conceived *a miracle* occurs. One more immortal soul is created by God.

Christian parents, for their part, invest their lives into the upbringing of their children. They work hard; they rearrange their priorities and their schedules. They make sacrifices so that one day the child may spread his or her wings, leave the nest and make a difference in our Church and in our world. Christian parents do this not expecting anything in return, but as a way of honoring God and giving thanks for the blessing of children. Christian parents bring children into the world not for reasons that are self-serving, but *to fulfill God's will.*

In this, Christian marriage is special. Christian marriage is not a mere contractual arrangement, but *a sacrament – a covenant* – through which the couple shares actively and intimately in the mission of Christ and His Church. This is why the family is called *the domestic church*, for it is in the family that

- *the Word of God is proclaimed and lived out;*
- *the virtues of charity and responsibility are fostered and encouraged; and*
- *God's love is made manifest.*

Christian parenthood is a beautiful example of stewardship. *God gives the gift of children according to His plan*, and for His reasons and purpose. Parents, you will *never* be fully aware of that purpose. But trust and pray that the Lord will bring to fulfillment the good work He and you have begun. *Persevere in prayer.* Persevere in your good works. Continue to be open to the Lord's will in your lives. Continue to be open to the gift of children. Be fruitful. Only the Lord knows the goodness that will enter into the world through your generosity.

Who is that good and faithful steward whom God will reward? The one who seeks the treasure that no thief can steal nor any moth destroy.[208] May our sharing in **the gift of the Eucharist, the gift more precious than silver or gold,**[209] help us to be good stewards of the many gifts God has given us. May God bless all Christian parents as they serve the Lord.

✠ **Nineteenth Week in Ordinary Time (C)**
August 9, 1998

Envy

Envy is a diabolical sin, one that separates us from God and neighbor. The remedy for the sin of envy is the practice of the virtues associated with stewardship: gratitude, responsibility, and generosity.

There is an urgency to the task at hand for the owner of the vineyard.[210] It is probably harvest time in the vineyard, a short window of opportunity for bringing in the grapes, just after they have ripened and just before they start to turn. The owner of the vineyard is looking for day laborers to assist his regular hired hands in the task of bringing in the harvest.

---

208 Cf. Luke 12:33.
209 Cf. 1 Peter 1:18.
210 Matthew 20:1-16a.

We are familiar with day laborers, aren't we? They eke out a living by doing the dirtiest, most grueling jobs. They are economically "on the edge." Often newly-arrived immigrants, they are so far from prosperity that their only hope, their only dream, is a better life for their children. They have to look out for one another and take care of one another. There is a natural solidarity among those who share the same lot in life, and there is great jubilation when one of their own "makes it" and climbs the ladder of success.

History recounts scores of injustices committed against the poor, for they have little defense against a greedy or unjust employer. The poor have had much about which to grumble down through the ages.

Jesus tells a different story today: He tells of an employer who is not only absolutely fair and just with all his employees, but also is incredibly generous with some – those hired late in the day. And of course, those hired first begin to grumble and murmur. Each of us would probably do the same. *It's human nature.* It's our way of looking at things.

And yet Jesus uses this parable to teach us about the Kingdom of God: *a kingdom in which God's justice is revealed,* a justice that far surpasses our human understanding, a *justice that overflows with the Lord's generosity, mercy and compassion.* "For my thoughts are not your thoughts, neither are your ways my ways," says the Lord. "For as the heavens are higher than the earth, so are my ways higher than your ways and my thoughts than your thoughts."[211] "Am I not allowed to do what I choose with what belongs to me?" asks the owner of the vineyard, "or do you begrudge my generosity?"[212] The master asks, "Am I not free to give a break to anyone who is economically on the edge? How are you deprived by my generosity?"

---

[211] Isaiah 55:8,9.
[212] Matthew 20:15.

"Why are you envious of another's good fortune?" Jesus would challenge us today. "Why are you so focused on what someone else has instead of considering first your own blessings?"

Jesus confronts *the sin of envy* – the sin that violates the Tenth Commandment: Thou shalt not covet thy neighbor's goods.[213] One of the seven deadly sins, St. Augustine went so far as to call envy "the diabolical sin."[214] St. Gregory the Great goes on to warn us, "*From envy are born* hatred, detraction, calumny, joy caused by the misfortune of a neighbor, and displeasure caused by his prosperity."[215]

Envy separates us from our neighbor. It divides us and pits us against one another which is exactly what the devil wants to see. The devil is the one who seeks to divide the flock so as to slaughter and destroy.[216]

Envy also separates us from God. When we are focused upon what someone else has, we can forget just how blessed we are. We can neglect to thank God for giving us our gifts and talents, our family, our friends, our health, and our very life. How sad that is! Though we might not have as much as someone else, and though the grass might seem so much greener on the other side of the fence, *we each have received blessings in abundance.* In fact, we have so many blessings that if we took the time to thank God for them we wouldn't have time to be envious!

Envy is a sadness. All sin, in fact, is a form of sadness, because sin leads us away from the good, away from God. Sin separates us from God and from one another.

---

[213] Cf. Exodus 20:17.
[214] Cf. St. Augustine, *De catechizandis rudibus* 4, 8: PL 40, 315-316; quoted in CCC 2539.
[215] St. Gregory the Great, *Moralia in Job* 31, 45: PL 76, 621; quoted in CCC 2539.
[216] Cf. John 10:10.

If you suffer from the sin of envy, *the remedy is to turn back to God and give Him thanks.* The antidote for envy is embracing the life of a steward, ever grateful for God's many gifts. Thank God daily for the abundant blessings that He showers upon you. List those blessings, thank Him for each one, and pledge to use those blessings for good rather than evil, to help rather than harm. If you are envious of your, sister, for example, thank God for blessing her so abundantly. Rejoice in your sister's good fortune and you will be giving glory to God, the source of all blessings.

Envy is a diabolical sin. It divides. It does the devil's work. *Gratitude and thanksgiving heal.* They unite. That is why the word for what we do here in this church every Sunday and every day is the word that means *thanksgiving.* That word, of course, is *Eucharist.*

We are spiritually impoverished. We are spiritually "on the edge" and so far from heaven that we can barely imagine what it will be like. Still, we offer our most profound thanks to God the Father for sending His Son Jesus into our world to free us from the shackles of sin and death. We offer thanks for the Holy Spirit who guides and directs us along the path that leads to heaven. We thank God for calling us to work in His vineyard and for promising a just wage for our efforts.

We would have nothing at all if it were not for *the generosity of God.* The good steward gives Him thanks today for all His blessings, especially for the blessing of the forgiveness of sins and the pledge of eternal life that is given to us every time we partake of *the Body and Blood of our Lord Jesus in the Eucharist.* This Sacrament of Unity, this Sacrament of Thanksgiving, is the sure and certain remedy against sin – especially the sin of envy.

☒ **The Twenty-fifth Sunday in Ordinary Time (A)**
September 19, 1999

Gratitude

The steward is known first and foremost by the mark of gratitude. "It is good to give thanks to the Lord, always and for everything."[217] The grateful heart wants for nothing, for you cannot be both grateful and unhappy at the same time.

The obvious theme of the Gospel today[218] is **gratitude.** Ten lepers are cured by Jesus, but the one who stands out among them is the one who returns, falls as the feet of Jesus and thanks Him.

Gratitude is a virtue, a virtue very much at the heart of our search for happiness in this world and in the next.

Let there be no mistake about it: **God wants us to be happy.** God has planted within each of our hearts a desire for happiness, a desire for a sense of well-being and contentment.[219] And while that desire for happiness can sometimes lead us toward an unhealthy preoccupation with material possessions, power, or pleasure, it also leads us directly to God, who alone can satisfy the hungry heart. **Things, status, and pleasure** may bring us momentary delight, but, as St. Augustine says, "Our heart is restless until it rests in you."[220]

Gratitude and happiness go together. "You cannot be grateful and unhappy at the same time."[221]

Believe it or not, scientific evidence supports this. Positive emotions such as gratitude and love have been shown to release endorphins into the bloodstream.

---

217 Cf. Psalm 92:1.
218 Luke 17:11-19.
219 Cf. CCC 1718.
220 St. Augustine, *Confessiones* 1,1,1: PL 32, 659-661; quoted in CCC 30.
221 *The Spirit of Well-Being,* a publication of St. Vincent Health Promotion Services; St. Vincent Health Care System, Indianapolis.

Endorphins are natural pain-killers in the body. So "the more we experience a sense of gratitude, the more endorphins and the less adrenaline we pump into our systems, thus contributing to longer, healthier lives. As we count our blessings, we literally bathe ourselves inwardly in good hormones."[222]

If gratitude is good for the body, it is even better for the soul. "It is good to give thanks to the Lord,"[223] the Psalmist says. "Give thanks in all circumstances,"[224] St. Paul exhorts us. *Expressing gratitude to God is one of the pillars of Christian prayer.* If someone is learning to pray, or if someone has forgotten how to pray, we can give no better advice to that person than to encourage him or her to be mindful of blessings received and to give God thanks for them. When we offer simple prayers of thanks to God for His blessings, often those simple prayers open our hearts to a deeper relationship with the Lord.

Gratitude is a mark of good stewardship, for the faithful steward never stops thanking God for blessings received.

We have so much for which to give thanks. *God has been so good to us.* And when we focus upon our blessings, when we consider just how kind God has been to us, we often find that the burdens we carry seem to be a bit lighter. When we deliberately count our blessings, the difficulties in life don't seem so daunting nor the challenges so complex. When we consider all that God has done for us, we can place our trust in Him to provide for us now and in the future.

God cares about us deeply. He is not remote or distant from our concerns. *He cares about us so much that He*

---

[222] Ibid.
[223] Psalm 92:1.
[224] 1 Thessalonians 5:18.

gave us His only Son, so "that whoever believes in Him should not perish but have eternal life."[225]

God shows His care for us without counting the cost. Jesus gives us everything He has to give by stretching out His arms on the cross. He is faithful to us even amidst our infidelity.

"If God is for us," St. Paul asks, "who is against us? He who did not spare His own Son but gave Him up for us all, will He not also give us all things with Him?"[226]

During this time of year when we renew our commitment to be good stewards, we rightly give thanks to God for ***the abundance of blessings*** that He showers upon us:

- the blessing of our family
- the blessing of material prosperity
- the blessing of our Catholic faith and parish
- the blessing of being loved
- the blessing of our health
- the blessing of our nation and the virtues for which our nations stands
- the blessing of the forgiveness of sins, the second chances that God gives us as we strive to be more wholehearted in living our faith.

We rightly count our blessings and give thanks. And when we do so sincerely, how can we be anything but happy?

We prepare now to enter more deeply into the great prayer of thanksgiving, ***the Eucharist.*** [227] In this great prayer we give thanks to the Lord for all that He has done for us, most especially His saving death and resurrection.

---

[225] John 3:16b.
[226] Romans 8:31,32.
[227] The Greek word for *thanksgiving* is *eucharistein*.

May we never stop giving thanks. May we never stop drawing near to the Holy Eucharist – the food and drink that is the Lord's Body and Blood, Soul and Divinity, the treasure worth **more than silver or gold,**[228] the bread of life and the cup of eternal salvation.

In giving thanks, and in receiving the Holy Eucharist, may we resolve to be even more committed to living **lives that bear witness to the magnanimous blessings** we have received.

✠ **The Twenty-eighth Sunday in Ordinary Time (C)**
October 14, 2001

"Master, I Want to See!"

The path of stewardship leads the steward to settle in life for nothing less than the fulfillment of the deepest desires of the soul: union with the Lord here on earth, and for all eternity.

The Gospel today[229] confronts us with two very important questions: **First,** what do you want out of life? **Second,** for what will you settle?

Most of us answer the first question with a single statement: *"I want to be happy."* It is fitting to strive for happiness, or "the good life" as it is called. And it is most appropriate that we should strive with all our being for eternal happiness – life forever with God in the communion of the saints.

What a tragedy to settle for anything less.

---

[228] Cf. 1 Peter 1:18.
[229] Mark 10:46-52, the account of the blind beggar, Bartimaeus.

Finding happiness can be **both simple and elusive**. Our senses often deceive us in our search for happiness. We get caught up in things that bring momentary pleasure but lead us into misery and unhappiness. Those who have followed the blind alleys of drugs, alcohol, or self-destructive relationships can attest to that. Similarly, our senses sometimes leave us feeling repulsed at doing those things that, in the end, bring us true peace and happiness. Many first-time parents have been anxious about the future sacrifices that would need to be made for their children, only later to discover great fulfillment in those experiences of parenthood.

An old adage is worth thinking about, especially as we enter into our annual stewardship renewal:

Material goods, when we do not have them,
   attract us.
Material goods, when we do have them,
   do not fulfill us.
Spiritual goods, when we do not have them,
   do not attract us.
Spiritual goods, when we do have them,
   fulfill our hearts' desire.

God gives us the gift of faith so that we might have insight into what will lead us to true happiness both in this world and in the next. **Faith is given to every human being,** although many of us pray as did the man in the Gospel: "I believe; help my unbelief!"[230] All of us have faith; all of us rightly pray for an increase in faith.

What is faith? **Faith is that deep inner longing for what is good, for what will make us truly happy.** And the greatest good, that which will make us truly happy, is the source of all goodness, **God himself.**

---

[230] Mark 9:24.

Bartimaeus was a man of true faith. Blind and a beggar, he never gave up on his heart's deepest desire. He never settled for anything less than the deepest longing of his heart.

Think about it: Jesus and *a large crowd* pass by Bartimaeus. He cries out, "Jesus, Son of David, have mercy on me."[231] Jesus stopped and asked Bartimaeus the same question he asks you and me: *"What do you want me to do for you?"*[232]

The blind beggar could have asked for material assistance, for had Jesus said the word the large crowd that was with him could have filled his beggar's cup to the brim. Perhaps one of the residents of Jericho would have taken Bartimaeus in, given him lodging and work to do. Jesus could have arranged that; he could have made it much easier for Bartimaeus to cope with his blindness.

But deep down in his heart that's not what Bartimaeus wanted. As a man of faith, as a man who believed that with God all things are possible, Bartimaeus answered Jesus' question quite frankly: "Master, I want to see!"[233]

Bartimaeus named his deepest longing and brought it to Jesus. And immediately, Bartimaeus' eyes were opened to a whole new life. Bartimaeus could see, and what is more important, he could see Jesus. And seeing Jesus, Bartimaeus would follow Him. He who once begged on the wayside would follow him who is the Way, the Truth, and the Life.[234]

Brothers and sisters, people of great faith, what do you want Jesus to do for you? *What is the deep desire of your heart?*

---

[231] Mark 10:47; In addressing Jesus as "Son of David", Bartimaeus acknowledges Jesus as the Savior, for the Messiah was to come from the lineage of King David.
[232] Mark 10:51.
[233] Cf. Mark 10:51.
[234] Cf. John 14:6.

May we never settle for anything less than the expression of faith contained in the words of Bartimaeus, "Master, I want to see!"

Master, I want to know Your will for my life. I want to experience Your forgiveness for all the sins that I have committed. I want to experience Your consoling presence as I face the struggles and sorrows of life. I want to follow You wherever You lead so that my life will not be wasted in selfishness but will be spent and poured out for the benefit of others and the upbuilding of the Kingdom of God.

Master, I want to see Your hand in everything I do, all in which I am involved, all upon which I spend my energy. Please, dear Master, grant that I may never hide myself from Your presence in shameful or dishonorable deeds.

Master, I want to know You here in this life through Your Word, through Your Sacraments, through the Holy Spirit, and through Your Body, the Church. And when my days are through, ***I want to see You*** for all eternity and live in Your presence for ages to come. Master, I want to see!

People of great faith, what do you want Jesus to do for you? Settle for nothing less than true happiness. ***Tell Jesus that you want to see.*** Turn to the Lord in prayer. Open your heart to Him and He will not disappoint you. Spend time regularly in prayer. Carve time out of your schedule for quiet prayer, for only in stillness before the Lord can you recognize what you truly need to find the happiness that the Lord has in store for you.

We pray each day for "our daily bread," ***the bread that is the mercy of the Lord in our lives.*** As we partake this day of the mercy that is the Holy Eucharist, may our eyes be opened to see in this Sacrament the gift that truly satisfies the hungry heart, that which brings us our ***lasting happiness and fulfills our hearts' desire.*** The good steward knows so well:

Material goods, when we do not have them,
   attract us.
Material goods, when we do have them,
   do not fulfill us.
Spiritual goods, when we do not have them,
   do not attract us.
Spiritual goods, when we do have them,
   fulfill our hearts' desire.

Please God, may we never settle for anything less.

✠ **The Thirtieth Sunday in Ordinary Time (B)**
October 29, 2000

Working Together as Stewards in the Church Community

Every parish is blessed by the steadfast dedication of its good stewards. "Many hands make light work" is a timeless adage whose truth is borne out in the practice of good stewardship of the gifts of time and talent.

The first reading[235] presents us with a scene that teaches a lesson about **working together.** Moses stands atop a high mountain with his arms outstretched in prayer so that the enemy down below might be defeated. As long as his arms are outstretched the battle goes well for the Israelites. But when fatigue sets in and his arms give way the tide of the battle turns.

How do the leaders of the people of Israel respond to this? They lend Moses a hand. Aaron and Hur each take an

---

[235] Exodus 17:8-13.

arm and allow Moses' prayer to continue in spite of his weariness.

Aaron and Hur do what they can so that the great prayers of Moses can go on. Because they were there, because of their efforts, the battle was won and the plan of God was advanced.

We can apply this lesson from the Bible to our efforts to be good stewards of the gifts God has given us, all for the sake of advancing the Kingdom of God. For whenever we use our talents, and whenever we give our time for the work of the Church, *we participate in the building of the Kingdom of God.*

Like Aaron and Hur, when we lend a hand at Church, even though it might not seem like we are doing a whole lot, we are, in fact, contributing to something much greater than ourselves. *When we choose*

- *to help rather than to stand idle ...*
- *to build up rather than to tear down ...*
- *to participate rather than letting someone else do the work*

... we advance the mission of the Church, just as our forebears taught us to do by their faith, their dedication, their commitment – their good stewardship of their time and talent.

We are blessed at St. Louis Parish with so many good stewards who lend their hands to the projects, activities, and ministries of the parish. Their efforts often go unheralded, but the Good Lord, who sees all things, will surely give them a fitting reward, for *God will not be outdone in generosity.*

At this time of year we engage in our annual renewal of stewardship of time, talent, and treasure. I thank those who have gotten involved. I commend those who do such extraordinary work and who work so well together. Their efforts in the Parish Festival (for example) speak for themselves: parishioners working together, each according to his or her ability, all so that the work of the Church might be advanced.

Every parish household will receive in the mail a list of ways to be involved in the life of the parish. I encourage you to consider this invitation prayerfully and to respond as best as you are able. *Every parishioner can do something.* Even many of our parishioners who are in nursing homes can be counted as good stewards, for some of our best *pray-ers* are listed as shut-ins. I assure you that their daily rosaries are of tremendous help to all of us who are engaged more visibly in the work of the Church.

Three particular opportunities stand out for special mention – things that you can do to help. There are specific things that need to be done if the work of the Church is to be accomplished.

First, the Helping Hands ministry is so important for those who need a hand in getting to the doctor or the grocery store, or who just need someone to listen to them kindly. We need workers for Helping Hands. We need some to be part of the leadership of this ministry, particularly those who are willing to spend one day each week fielding the calls that come in, serving as dispatchers, as it were.

Second, our community food pantry is operated by the various churches in town. Every congregation takes one month to fill the pantry with groceries and to staff it. Because our church is the largest, we are given the busiest month – the month that includes Thanksgiving Day (November). Your help is needed as the poor depend on our care and our help.

Finally, we have great hopes for our Youth Ministry program. Volunteers are needed to chaperone events and to help with some of the paperwork. If you can lend a hand in this area we will be able to do so much more than we are already doing.

Presently, we are blessed with many good stewards of time and talent, yet we need more stewards to join in their efforts. I encourage you to **consider prayerfully** the mailing you will receive, and to be attentive to the pleas for help that are made throughout the year in the bulletin and at announcement time.

Many hands make light work, and the arms of some of most dedicated stewards are growing weary. I know you will do your best to lend a hand.

We prepare now to enter into the Liturgy of the Eucharist. We prepare to draw near to the Lord Jesus, who, like Moses, **stretches out His arms between heaven and earth on the high mountain of Calvary**, all so that the enemy might be defeated and that we might have life and have it to the full.[236]

✠ **The Twenty-ninth Sunday in Ordinary Time (C)**
October 17, 2004

Let Go, Let God

Stewardship of treasure is a consciousness about what we own. More importantly, it is often a sober reminder of what owns us. The good steward learns time and again the wisdom of entrusting his or her material possessions to the service of the Lord.

Zaccheus was a wealthy man, but he was miserable. He was hated by everyone because he obtained his money

---

[236] Cf. John 10:10.

by extortion and trickery. He was a tax collector to be sure, but he didn't just collect taxes. He took his cut as well – enough to make him so wealthy that he was miserable.

When Jesus enters his life Zaccheus re-evaluates everything. He changes his priorities. He lets go of his ill-gotten wealth and gives it to the poor. And in letting go of all that he had previously clung to so tenaciously, Zaccheus finds freedom and happiness – in this world and the next.

The message of the Gospel today[237] is *let go, let God and see what happens.*

There was once a small village that was troubled by a very pesky monkey. That monkey was into everything and was causing quite a disruption in the life of the village. The chief put a bounty on the monkey's head and all the men in the village tried to catch it. Day after day they tried, but the monkey always seemed to evade them.

One day one of the oldest men in the village, frail and arthritic, showed up with the monkey on a leash. "How did you do it?" they all asked him. "You are all hobbled over with your aches and pains. How did you catch the same monkey that had been evading much more agile men?"

So he showed them how he had done it. He had woven a small basket, covered on all sides, and mounted it to his porch. In the basket he hung a banana. Now the slats in the basket were large enough so that the monkey could slide in his open hand, but when the monkey grabbed the banana, his clenched fist was too big to squeeze through those same slats.

The monkey could either hold on to the banana and risk capture by the elderly villager, or he could let go and run free. The foolish monkey failed to let go of the banana and so surrendered his freedom.

---

[237] Luke 19:1-10.

Let go, let God and see what happens. That's the
message of the Gospel. That's the message of this little story.
That's the message of stewardship as a way of life.

What is the banana in your life? What are you holding on
to at the expense of your true freedom? ***What do you need
to let go of?*** Is it stubbornness with a grudge that you have
been holding for too long? Is it selfishness that takes
precedence over spending time with those who need you? Is
it stinginess with money?

What do you need to let go of in order to be free?
That's the lesson of the Gospel and that's what we're talking
about every time we bring up the subject of Stewardship.
What do we own and what owns us?

I once knew a gentleman whose career was on the rise.
He also had a lovely family, a good wife, and three wonderful
children all under the age of ten. They loved their daddy and
loved spending time with him.

He finally got the promotion that he had been praying
for, so he moved his family to New York where he found a
good salary with all the benefits and even more ladder-
climbing ahead of him.

But six months after his move he called me. His job
required of him much more travel than he had thought. His
kids hardly saw him. And they missed their grandparents and
their friends. He was wealthy beyond his dreams but was also
quite miserable.

He told me that he had a decision to make: to stay in
New York or to take a voluntary demotion and move back
home. He told me that he had been praying about it and that
the word that kept coming to his mind was ***stewardship.
Let go. Let God. And see what happens.***

Within six weeks he arranged a transfer back home --
with a big cut in salary. But he and his family could not have

been happier and to this day he has no regrets. He let go of what he **thought** would make him happy and experienced the freedom that comes with **true happiness.**

The good steward of time, talent, and treasure decides to let go, let God, and see what happens.

Later this week you will receive in the mail your annual intention card. I encourage you to consider prayerfully how you will share your gifts of time, talent, and treasure: how you will let go of those gifts for the sake of building up the Kingdom of God.

I have already spoken of time and talent. Today I speak of **treasure.**

You might recall that I promised to speak from the pulpit about parish finances no more than once a year. Well, it's been about a year. Thank you for helping me to keep that promise.

Let me thank you for your offertory gifts last year. We finished the last fiscal year well ahead of budget, and we were able to use our surplus to put new windows in the school and accomplish a number of other improvements. Thank you for your sacrifices.

Let me ask you to consider this year a prayerful, proportionate and sacrificial gift. **Prayerful** – because all things are from the Lord. **Proportionate** – because we do not want to give the same amount every year.[238] I invite you to join me in giving at the **10% level.** 5% to the parish. 1% to the United Catholic Appeal.[239] And 4% to charities of your choice.

Prayerful. Proportionate. **Sacrificial.** Only you know what a sacrificial gift is for you. For me, it's a gift that means

---

[238] When giving proportionately, our gift amount could go up or down in a particular year.
[239] The annual fund for the Archdiocese of Indianapolis.

something – a gift that I feel when I give it. *A sacrificial gift makes a difference, both in the one who is giving and for the one who is receiving it.*

Please consider prayerfully how you are called to respond to the growing needs of our church – here in the parish and out in the wider Church. Your intention card has three parts; part one is for our archdiocesan United Catholic Appeal. Parts two and three are for our parish needs: the former applies to your commitment of time and talent, and the latter to your commitment of treasure. It would be most helpful to have the cards returned in the collection or to the parish office in the next three weeks.

In returning your card you are signaling your desire to be part of the good work of the Church. You are building up the Kingdom by helping us to continue to teach the faith, reach out to the less fortunate, and provide for the needs of the Church.

As we participate in the Holy Eucharist this day – as we draw near to the Lord Jesus who gave everything He had to give so that we might have life to the full – may we be inspired in our stewardship to *let go, let God, and see what happens.*

✠ **The Thirty-first Sunday in Ordinary Time (C)**
October 31, 2004

A Final Word ...

I hope that these pages have helped you to understand more about *stewardship as a way of life.* Throughout Her history, the Church has been built up by good and faithful stewards, the most well-known of whom we honor with the title *saint.* Stewardship is a way of *sanctity,* a way of *holiness,* for it is *a spirituality of gratitude and responsibility* for the spiritual and material gifts that God has bestowed upon us. Stewardship is a way of life that has the power to *renew the Church and evangelize the culture,* because it compels the steward to share generously of those same spiritual and material gifts.

If you want to learn more about stewardship, I encourage you to read the pastoral letter of the Bishops of the United States, *Stewardship: A Disciple's Response.* The letter is the bishops' best selling pastoral letter, probably because it is easy to read and it has questions for reflection and discussion at the end of each chapter. Most importantly, its message resonates within the hearts of nearly everyone who reads it.

To go further, I encourage you to become acquainted with the *International Catholic Stewardship Council* (ICSC, www.catholicstewardship.org). ICSC is preeminent in promoting stewardship as a way of life. Its publications, conferences, and institutes are most helpful in forming good stewards. Many parishes and dioceses are members of ICSC.

Above all, *be committed to the practice of fervent prayer and faithful participation in the sacraments of the Church.* Great things happen when one draws close to the Lord, asking with an open heart, "Lord, what do You want me to do to serve Your Church?" The Lord is good about

177

answering those prayers, and *He will not be outdone in generosity.*

May God bless you and keep you always in His love. And when your days on earth are finished and you are asked to render an account of your stewardship, may the good Lord smile upon you and say, "Well done, good and faithful steward. Come and share your Master's joy."

Index

This index is not meant to be exhaustive, but presents the individuals and major themes within *More than Silver or Gold.* Page numbers refer to the first page of each homily.

Acknowledgments

Excerpts from *Vatican Council II, Volume I: The Conciliar and Postconciliar Documents, New Revised Edition*, Austin Flannery, OP, general editor; © 1975, 1986, 1992, 1996 by Reverend Austin Flannery, OP; Permissions for extractions administered by Costello Publishing Company, Northport, NY. Used with permission.

Excerpts from the English translation of *The Rite of Marriage* © 1969, International Committee on English in the Liturgy, Inc. (ICEL); the English translation of *The Rite of Baptism*, © 1969, ICEL; the English translation of the Confessions of St. Augustine from *The Liturgy of the Hours* © 1974, ICEL. All rights reserved. Used with permission.

Excerpt from the *Denver Catholic Register* / Archdiocese of Denver, April 28, 1999. Used with permission.

Excerpt from *The Catholic Answers Guide to Family Finances* by Philip Lenahan, p. 1; © 2000, Catholic Answers. (www.catholic.com) Used with permission.

Excerpt from the *Baton Rouge Advocate*, "Scalia: Faithful Live for Christ" by Penny Brown Roberts; January 23, 2005; © 2005, Capital City Press. Used with permission.

Excerpt from "Honor Life with Gratitude," *The Spirit of Well-Being*, a publication of St. Vincent Health Promotion Services, Indianapolis. Used with permission.

The editor and publisher are grateful to all copyright holders without whose material this book could not have been completed. If in any circumstance proper acknowledgment is lacking, please notify Saint Catherine of Siena Press so that future printings of this work may be corrected.

SAINT CATHERINE OF SIENA PRESS

What are we all about?

Good things happen when Catholics get together to study and to pray – provided they are using resources that are orthodox and holy. Unfortunately, such materials have been in short supply – and **Saint Catherine of Siena Press is responding** to this with quality resources for adult Catholics.

We take legitimate pride in publishing materials that put the reader in contact with the truths of the faith: The Holy Bible, the Fathers of the Church, papal and conciliar documents, the Catechism of the Catholic Church, and contemporary Catholic authors.

Our first publication, **A Study Guide to Living the Catholic Faith,** is a companion volume to *Living the Catholic Faith*, by Archbishop Charles Chaput, OFM Cap. of Denver. Check out our website to learn more about the Study Guide and how to use it in small group or individual study.

Our patroness, Saint Catherine of Siena, is a Doctor of the Church and the Patron Saint of Italy. A member of the Third Order of St. Dominic, she labored untiringly and with fiery zeal for the unity of the Church and was a devoted champion of the Papacy

www.saintcatherineofsienapress.com

888-232-1492